PRAISE for *And These Are the Good Times*

"Patricia Ann McNair's *And These Are the Good Times* is a startlingly evocative exploration of the complexities of family, love, writing, sex, loss, and national identity. McNair's essays are challenging, colloquial, and contemplative. Her work recalls Jo Ann Beard and Mary Karr in its powerful insistence and range."

—Joe Meno, author of *Marvel and a Wonder* and *Hairstyles of the Damned*

"'Good,' in the dexterous eyes and mind of Patricia Ann McNair, lodges itself in the details. A safety-pinned button on the cuff of a Cuban valet's fresh uniform; the cool relief of Thin Mints after the flu; Christmas interpreted by a 400-pound cab driver. These essays travel widely through time and geography, and all are places and moments you'll count yourself lucky to have ventured with a wry, smart yet tender-hearted guide. McNair searches for home, and finds homes instead."

—Mardi Jo Link, author of *Bootstrapper: From Broke to Badass on a Northern Michigan Farm*

"The essays in *And These Are the Good Times* are so arrestingly good that I had to stop several times to marvel at how keen, generous, and compassionate Patricia Ann McNair's writing is. She's put her arms around the world and embraced so many of its complexities with the great heart and wondering eye of a poet."

—Christine Sneed, author of *Little Known Facts* and *The Virginity of Famous Men*

D0291277

Also by Patricia Ann McNair: *The Temple of Air*

AND THESE ARE THE GOOD TIMES

A Chicago gal riffs on death, sex, life, dancing, writing, wonder, loneliness, place, family, faith, coffee, and the FBI (among other things)

PATRICIA ANN McNAIR

A SIDE STREET PRESS BOOK

Published by
Side Street Press Inc.
3400 West 111th Street, #412
Chicago, IL 60655

www.sidestreetpressinc.com

Copyright: Patricia Ann McNair, 2016

ISBN: 978-0-9988039-0-6

Library of Congress Control Number: 2017943459

Printed in the United States of America

First Edition: September, 2017

Cover by Patrick Foley

For Philip
And in memory of Sizzle, Mac, and Roger the Dodger

DEATH, SEX, LIFE, AND DANCING

WRITING, WONDER, LONELINESS, AND PLACE

FAMILY, FAITH, COFFEE, AND THE FBI (AMONG OTHER THINGS)

AND THESE ARE THE GOOD TIMES

A Chicago gal riffs on death, sex, life, dancing, writing, wonder, loneliness, place, family, faith, coffee, and the FBI (among other things)

DEATH, SEX, LIFE,
AND
DANCING

AND THESE ARE THE GOOD TIMES

My father didn't believe in jukeboxes. I swear to God. "Damned things are all part of the syndicate," he'd say. When I was ten, I didn't know what the syndicate was. I knew the word somehow, knew of it: *The Dick Van Dyke Show* was in syndication, *Father Knows Best*, too. But the word didn't fit for me here.

"The mob," one or another of my brothers explained. Mob was a word I did know. I was from just outside Chicago, after all. Jimmy Hoffa was still alive. I had this picture in my mind of some guy in a dark suit and hat pushing the jukebox away from the wall at Sullivan's — the tavern around the corner — and opening some magic door in the back of the machine and a whole silvery stream of coins would rush out into his leather satchel. He'd close it all up when the stream went dry, push the jukebox back flush against the wall, maybe touch the sharp brim of his fedora or nod to Mr. Sullivan behind the bar and walk out of the darkness into the day, the door swinging shut behind him.

My dad hated the mob. They were dangerous in ways that I couldn't even begin to understand, always behind something or other that was wrong with society, he said. Drugs. Prostitution. Jukeboxes. Dad had been an early union rabble-rouser, a card-carrying Communist, and even as a kid I knew that the mob was the enemy of men like him. Sullivan's was his hangout. Half of the place was a package liquor store, a place where you could get milk, coffee, dishwashing liquid, bread, a six-pack of Schlitz, a pint of Jim Beam. With fifty-five cents and a note from my mom, I could go in and pick up a pack of Kents. The other half, on the opposite side of low-slung doors, was the bar. I spent a lot of time in that bar. We've all read these stories about little kids having to face the darkness of smelly taverns in order to drag their drunken mothers, their drunken fathers home, the kids hating the whole thing. But it wasn't like that for me. Sure, sometimes my mom would send me to pick up a loaf of bread for dinner, and I'd have to round up Dad while I was there. Other times I'd go there on my own when he wasn't home before dark. Still other times my dad would call the house from the payphone there and invite us all to join him. Mom might or might not go. Don and Allen were in high school and too old, too cool to be hanging out with their family. Roger (twelve, two years older than I) probably was unwilling to turn off the television. But I'd go. I wanted to be there. I'd make my way down our street past the other clipped lawns and split-levels, past the hardware store with the three apartments above it, past the hot dog stand where in just a couple of years I'd sit at one of the red picnic tables and make out with a boy for the first time, and around the corner to Sullivan's. There I'd push through the swinging doors, leave behind the bright lights and dusty shelves of the store, and step into the smoky darkness of the tavern.

Dad, in a suit coat and tie from a day at the office in the Loop (having given up his causes in order to support his family), always sat at the bar, a beer in one hand, a cigarette in the other. He told stories and jokes to whomever would listen. "There were these two deaf-mutes…" (it was the sixties, remember) and he'd wave his hands wildly in some made-up, exaggerated sign language, ashes from his cigarette floating in the air, peppering the bright white front of his shirt. He'd order a round for his audience, "the usual" for himself. He'd talk as long as they'd listen. But sometimes there'd be no one to entertain, so he'd sit by himself and chew the inside of his mouth and squint through the smoke into the open space in front of him like he was looking for something, like he was working to figure something out.

When the tavern was crowded, I'd squeeze into a self-made slot next to my dad, push up against the consid-erable bulk of him. Six feet tall and 200-plus pounds, Dad made a good lean-to. When there was an empty spot, I'd lift myself onto the vinyl barstool, slide my elbows over the counter, ask for a Coke or a Squirt. "The usual," he'd say and get a shot and a beer for himself. My dad would buy me sodas and Beer Nuts and put his hand on the back of my neck. I liked the way it felt, this bellying up to the bar. I'd watch the plastic sky-blue waters ripple across the Hamm's beer sign over the bar and admire the long elegant neck of the Galliano bottle that stood next to the shorter, clumsier bottles of house brands. I'd pretend not to while I listened to my dad telling a joke in a stage whisper to the guy next to him, try to memorize the way it went from traveling salesman to farm girl to the punch line so I could tell it to my brothers or my best friend later. It never mattered to me that most times I was the only kid there. I guess in a place like that, surrounded by grown-ups smoking and laughing and talking grown-up talk, I imagined I was something other than a kid myself.

And there was the jukebox. The flashing lights, the automatic arm flipping 45s onto the turntable. I'd watch the discs spin under the needle and I'd pore over the titles on the tiny slips of cardboard. G5... "Lemon Tree". H7... "Mr. Lonely". K8... "Action". The jukebox stood where most jukeboxes do, next to the bathrooms. I suppose bar people knew that sometimes there'd be a line there, and those waiting were apt to pump money into the box. Or maybe the mob figured this out.

I'd lean on the juke, rest my palms on the glass, and look over my shoulder to my dad, hoping he'd get the hint. Sometimes I'd walk back and forth between the box and him and sing along with the songs. But he just wouldn't get it. Finally, I'd have to ask for some money. I knew how he felt about jukeboxes, knew that he would tell me again: "Putting money in that box is like handing it right to the syndicate. My pocket to theirs." But then he'd let loose a heavy sigh, clench his cigarette in the grip of his teeth, and reach into the jingle of his pocket where there was always a ton of change and junk. He'd pull up a handful of the stuff and dump it on the bar where I'd pick through the tobacco and buttons and lint for the dimes. And I'd take all I could over to the jukebox, where I gave my dad's money to his enemy. The thing is, he let me.

I'd play something fast, imagine myself on *American Bandstand* or *Hullabaloo* and dance to the jukebox by myself. Women in pantsuits and high hair, women I never noticed anywhere in the neighborhood but here, would pass me on their way to the bathroom and tell me how good I was. Guys in sport jackets or shirtsleeves and ties or uniforms with their names sewn over the pockets would go by and say "Nice moves," and "Shake it, baby."

Older guys. Guys as old as my dad.

I remember this one time. It was the kind of Chicago summer evening when the air hangs thick and unmoving and the sun takes its own sweet time going down, that kind of bright, hot early night that you're grateful to get out of—even if it's to be inside a bar with no air conditioning. Because at least it's dark in there, and the darkness seems cool, especially when someone opens the door and the hot light of the slowly setting sun stings your eyes, heats up your skin. It was one of those nights when Mr. Sullivan plugged in the huge, old, freestanding fan and the tables closest to it filled up fast. The jukebox was right there, too, and I could feel the mechanical breeze blow against the back of my neck while I danced. It was the fan that brought the crowd to that side of the bar, I'm pretty sure now, but then I thought it must have been me. Those older guys leaned on the bar and watched me, or they sat around low tables and slapped their hands in time with the music on the wood tops. Sometimes they'd shovel a few dimes into the box and tell me to pick out whatever I wanted to hear, whatever I wanted to dance to. A man I'd never seen there before, thick dark hair and sweat rings under the arms of his striped golf shirt, slurred something to me as he went past. I didn't get it, but he smiled drunkenly and said it again: "Give it to me, girly." I, always the star, smiled back at the man and even as his date, a bleached blond, blue-eyeshadowed woman in red yanked him away from me, I went on dancing. I could see my dad from there, watched him and the wavy reflection of him in the grimy mirror behind the bar as he made his arm into the trunk of an elephant for the punch line of one of his jokes, watched him slap a palm on the bartop when he laughed, watched him run a hand over his VO5-slicked comb over and then throw back one of the small glasses of whiskey and draw his lips away from his teeth, wrinkle up his nose. And when no one was around him, when no one was listening, I saw him slump inside his coat, his bigness shrinking some, his eyes squinting into the space in front of him.

I don't know if he ever watched me, but every night I wished he would. That's why I kept my eyes on him while I jumped around and spun in circles and twisted back and forth. I'm not sure what I wanted him to see in me. Maybe I hoped he'd recognize the same thing I saw in him when he told his stories, a need for that devoted attention, a desire for a certain appreciation. Maybe I just hoped we could dance together. But when he'd push himself up from the bar and walk to the bathroom, pass by me, he'd look at me like it was a surprise to see me there dancing in the dark, being cheered on by a few strangers. He'd reach out and cup my chin, let his hand trail across my cheek, and then he'd keep walking to the men's room. I felt the pull of his hand on me. I wanted to follow him, to move in such a way that his palm stayed pressed against my cheek. But he'd walk on, his hands to himself again, and the door would swing closed behind him.

All of this was before I got to be too cool to be seen with my parents, before I'd rather be with kids my own age and did most of my dancing at parties with my girl-friends or sweaty-palmed boys a head shorter than I, before my dad suffered a heart attack one night on his way home from work and died when he was fifty-five and I was just fifteen. Too many cigarettes, probably, and too much booze. Mostly, though, he had a weak heart, a family ailment that took one of his brothers, and more recently, one of mine.

And even though it's been decades since Dad died, not a year goes by when I don't remember how I could talk him out of his dimes, and the dances I'd buy with them. I remember how it felt to sit high on a barstool next to my father, and I remember the crackling cellophane bags of Beer Nuts we passed back and forth to share. I especially remember the soft warmth of his big hand on my neck, the cup and pull of his palm on my cheek.

Maybe it was that same pull that brought me to a different bar two years after his death. Away at college, I'd leave my early morning freshman comp class and walk down Main Street to Joe's, where they served twofers (two-for-one drinks) from 10:30 until 4:00. It was a place not unlike Sullivan's, smoky and dark with beer signs and Beer Nuts, but this was a small town bar with pickled eggs and pigs' knuckles in huge jars of brine where the Galliano should be, and it was hard to be there for any length of time without somebody playing that song about Lucille and the fine time she picked to leave. Even so, it became my place. And the regulars — Gene, the pickled-up farmer, a wrinkly guy in coveralls who drank shots of blackberry brandy; Ernie, a maintenance man from school, complete with uniform, who was partial to shells of PBR; Dorothy, a woman fond of Black Velvet and Coke and white silk blouses, a woman who danced the twist no matter what I'd play on the jukebox — would buy me drinks, and I'd buy for them.

A couple of years after that, when I went to rehearsals at the community theater located on the bad side of a small Iowa city, I found myself pulled across the street to a neighborhood place whenever I had time between my scenes. I'd order a vodka and grapefruit, talk to the bartender and the union guys — grubby and stinking from the packing plant down the street — and pick a song or two off the jukebox. After opening night of the play, the cast and crew went across the street to celebrate, and the bartender called out my name. "The usual, Patty?" The other cast members swiveled their heads to stare. "The usual?" they said. I nodded and smiled, loaded up the jukebox with coins and selections so we could dance all night if we wanted to. I was twenty-one and a regular, drinking my usual in a sticky-floored, smoke-filled tavern with a bunch of working folks. It was as close to home as I could get.

All through my twenties I worked in bars: waitressing, tending, managing. For years I'd hang out in them, and for years I'd dance in them. Only I didn't grow up to be a drunk, and I didn't grow up to be a stripper. I just grew up. As I write this, 1998, I'm closer to forty now than thirty, closer to my dad's age when he died than I am to my own when I lost him. I have a real job now in a college just a few blocks from where my father's office was in the Loop, and a husband. I have less time and — let's face it — less energy than I used to. But every once in a while I'll find myself in a tavern for some reason, maybe to use the phone or the bathroom, maybe to meet a friend or grab a beer with a co-worker. It's never Sullivan's, though it might as well be. Sullivan's isn't Sullivan's anymore. It's still there, but different. Painted bright white outside and in, they serve meals on tables covered with oilcloth, and the jukebox is gone. Still, in this other tavern, I get that same feeling from way back then. That time, that place. It's that sweet, I'm-home feeling. And I'm pulled to the jukebox. I read the titles, shovel in quarters and dollars. I stand with my friends and bounce on the balls of my feet. I want to dance, but — I'm sorry to say — like most adults, I've grown too controlled, too stodgy to let loose so easily.

And at these places there is always some guy, some older guy (as old as my dad was when he died), sitting at the bar telling stories, being charming, buying drinks, getting drunk. He's someone's father, I'll bet. Sometimes he's with his wife, but usually she leaves early, leaves him behind so he has to stumble home on his own. He doesn't seem to notice when she's gone. I'll slip in next to the guy, order my drink, smile at him. Sometimes we'll talk. How's it going? Having fun? The bartender will watch and roll his eyes at me while the guy slurs over his answers and drops ashes down the front of this shirt. Sometimes the guy'll buy me a drink. Sometimes I'll buy him one.

When I'm at the jukebox, he'll slide by on his way to the bathroom, or maybe he'll follow me to the machine to give me money to play something. Anything. My choice. A single play is at least a quarter; nothing costs a dime these days. And I wonder if the syndicate still owns the jukeboxes now that they take real money, dollars and fives. There are different titles now ("All I Wanna Do", "Time After Time"), and still some of the same ("Lemon Tree", "Mr. Lonely".) The discs are compact, no longer the wax ones you could watch fall into place and spin under the long arm with its needle. You can't quite see how it works anymore.

Then sometimes, and these are the good times, the man will nod or bow a little bow. "Dance?" he'll ask, and reach a hand out to me. And I'll slide my hand into his, feel its warmth, marvel at its softness. And I'll step close to him as the music fills in the space and time around us, and I'll look up into the face of someone's father.

"I thought you'd never ask," I'll say.

And then, finally, we'll dance.

WHAT YOU'LL REMEMBER

You sit in the back of the cab, a white boxy thing you think of as Soviet-made, you don't know why, and the oily fumes come in through the windows on hot, wet air that barely moves. Your guide stretches forward and speaks a stream of words to the driver, soft, in that voice you like to lean in close to hear, to feel the breath on the skin of your face, your neck. And you wonder how the driver can possibly make anything out over the unmuffled motor. Only he does, and he smiles and glances back in his rearview, looks right at you, into your eyes. His own those particular Cuban eyes, the light ones, green or gray or blue (sometimes gold) and rimmed black around the iris—and you feel your chest tighten a little like it always does when you see those eyes, and you smile back at the driver who says something fast and blurry, a question it sounds like, and you nod even though you don't understand but it seems like he might have asked "¿Bien viaje?" or something like that, something you suspect means "Good trip?"

And your guide laughs. He pats the man on the shoulder and leans back into the seat beside you, close to you because the vinyl on his side is torn and a spring pushes up and out of it, silver and sharp looking. And his door has no handle. So the two of you press together, sharing your side. You don't mind; his arm is hard against your sunburned one, the skin cooler than yours. He puts a hand on your thigh in that way you notice Cubans touch, sure and flat-palmed, not like back home in Chicago where strangers touch one another like it's an accident, with fingertips or the bony backs of their hands. You remember how just a few days ago you stood in the crowd at the rumba concert in the alley painted bright with murals and scattered with sculptures made from metal and wood and things that once were something else, buckets and bicycle tires and bathtubs, and you felt a hand on your waist. One whole hand pressed against you, and another one low on your shoulder blade. You thought for just a moment that it must be a friend there, only you knew it couldn't be, not possibly. You were on your own, your colleagues gone back to the States while you stayed on, alone in Havana now that the conference was over. You figured what the hell. Your life had gone black and white; you were forty and newly alone and even though it was a brand new century, nothing ever changed. And now you wanted something you could carry away with you back to your too-big apartment in the city, something that when you opened it up to look at again, your life would fill up with color. Something to remember. You were surprised how easy it all was, changing your return tickets, paying for the room in advance, just like any old trip, even though you ached for something new. And so at the concert in the painted alley, you leaned into the hands, let them touch you: "*Permiso*," the man you'd never seen before (small, dark, kind-looking) said, and you said: "*Es suyo*." All he wanted was permission to pass, but still, you let him move you, and after, long after, you remember leaning into those hands.

"Give me five dollars," your guide says, hand still on your knee, and you realize (more than a little disappointed) that he means nothing by the hand, he's just making contact to get your attention. Hatuey his name is, and you remember how it took almost an hour for you to get it close to right. You loved listening to his voice while he said it, the *H* barely a breath; you loved watching him repeat it, his lips pursed and opened, his tongue gentle on his teeth to release the *T*. "Hot-too-way," you said, and finally he nodded and shrugged like "close enough" and smiled. And you flinched a little at his smile, the teeth dark and ragged in his smooth, twenty-eight-year-old face. But then you found yourself saying the name under your breath, even after he'd left you in the bar where you met, and then while you rode the elevator to your floor, your room, the sewer smell from the basement following you up and up. And when you awoke the next morning and looked out your window to the apartments across the way, heard the rooster crowing somewhere beneath you from the streets of Havana, saw the green-and-yellow parrot in a cage on an opposite balcony, you remembered the name and whispered it again and again. *Hatuey Hatuey Hatuey.* And it sounded good.

In the taxi, you dig in your pocket and pull out a five, U.S., and you're amused that the meter reads U.S. dollars, and how most things you've bought you've paid for in dollars, and how the Cubans have minted coins and printed pesos that are equal to dollars to give tourists change back. And you wonder, not for the first time since you landed at the Havana airport in a crowd of dozens of other Americans (musicologists from Harvard, Baptists from the Carolinas, blond kids from a midwestern high school), how the embargo can possibly be effective if everywhere you go the place is filled with U.S. money? The taxi turns down another street, and you leave behind the dark residential block, move away from the huge concrete mansions that have been partitioned and divided up into multi-family dwellings. In the dark you could almost imagine what the street must have looked like forty years ago: ornate balconies and stained-glass windows and courtyards lined with bright ceramic tiles and planted with palm trees. You've seen it in the light, though; the sidewalks are cracked and the salt air has worn the walls through in places, and wash hangs on lines stretched from one palm to another. Gray sheets and faded flower-print dresses and shoes hang from the iron bars over the windows, airing out. You've seen more than one courtyard strewn with broken concrete, and you've seen another with a goat tethered to a post by a rope.

Now you are on a different street. A wide boulevard with billboards painted with story-high faces and slogans underneath. "*Patria o Muerte*" under black-bearded Fidel. "*Recordamos Siempre*" under Che in his beret. And under the innocent face of that little boy held hostage by his relatives in Miami, words demanding his return. You're turned around some now, from the taxi ride and from the rum you started drinking in the patio bar at your hotel while you waited for Hatuey. You know that the ocean is out there somewhere, to your right maybe, a block away, two at the most. Hotels on this boulevard are huge and bright and recently painted, the driveways wide and paved smooth, the parking lots full of new cars from Japan and old, old cars from the States. Your smoking, stinking, grumbling taxi pulls into one of the driveways and follows the curves until you reach a doorway with a concrete awning that boasts *Café Havana* in big, black script. A valet trots to your door and wrestles it open, and you notice how even though his uniform is clean and pressed (bright red jacket, sleek black pants), a safety pin holds a button to his cuff, and the pants are too short and marked by the lines of hems let down and sewn up over and over again. Hatuey gives the cabbie the five and puts a hand out for the change, but you wave it away and say, "Keep it," and even though it's English you've spoken, the man understands and turns his beautiful Cuban eyes to you and says, "*Gracias.*" "*Por nada,*" you remember to say.

In the foyer the sign reads in English, "$12.50 table" and "$7.00 bar/stand" and "First Drink FREE." You're in front of Hatuey and the music from inside the club is so loud you can feel it, the thrum of the bass moves through you so when Hatuey reaches out and draws his knuckle up your spine — starting at the small of your back, moving up between your shoulder blades where your skin is exposed and stinging with sunburn, to the nape of your neck — you feel yourself lean back into his touch. But then you remember who you are, boss and hired help, and you step forward and out of reach. "*Nosotros,*" you say to the cashier at the door and hand her fourteen dollars, and then you're in the club and on your way to an open seat at the bar and the air conditioning is cranked and it's the first time since you've been in Cuba that you've felt cold.

When Hatuey catches up, you're already ordering, but he signals the waiter and orders scotch, Johnny Walker Red, and when you open your mouth to protest, he says, "We pay good money. We take good drink." You want to tell him that you can get Johnny Walker Red anytime at home, and the truth is it's not all that good. What you want is a *mojito*, Havana Club white rum and limes and sugar and mint: you can't get those at home, not like here, bars make them, but they are not the same. But you let Hatuey have his way this time, and when you lift the drink to your lips the brown liquor burns at first (you've gotten used to the fresh, sweet stuff), but then it tastes better than you expected and it goes down easy. So you have another.

By the time you turn around and get a good look at the club, you're pretty tipsy, and you try not to laugh at how tacky the place is. The worst of the eighties (even though it's a whole new century), Hard Rock Cuba or something. Old American cars polished up and standing on platforms, twirling disco lights, a flashing dance floor, and a stage show with audience participation and men in white suits and Panama hats making jokes you can't translate but are pretty sure are silly and old and not at all funny, even though everyone laughs and cheers and pumps their fists in the air. It's nearly all tourists: middle-agers in good dresses and sharply creased trousers (Brits, you think, or maybe Canadians); young, probably newly-wed Asians who sit close together and look slightly frightened; more Americans than you'd have expected, mostly single women in their thirties, their forties, in little sundresses with spaghetti straps and bare legs and high-heeled sandals (you're glad you wore jeans and a silk blouse), their hair down and their faces tanned; their escorts (young, handsome Cuban men, men like Hatuey) whisper in their ears and pull them out to dance. And the others. Older white men with dyed hair or fake hair and cigars, big and round and phallic, their meaty hands on the shoulders of the little Cuban girls (teenagers, really) they will be paying for the date.

You can't help but wonder over the Cubans. Not the

escorts and the dates, but those who roam the club: men in tight white pants and shirts open to show flesh and muscle, young women in velour cat suits and short, short dresses. The cover charge is nearly one-fourth of what any single national is allowed to make in a month, so you know they must be out for more than a good time, there must be some payoff here. Trolling for tourists, maybe, like how Hatuey approached you at the hotel bar, bought you a *cerveza nacional*, offered in his quiet, deep voice to show you around for just ten dollars a day and expenses. *Jineteros*, they call these guys, a word you don't know the exact translation of, but suspect falls somewhere between vendor and hooker.

A thick man pushes a girl up to the bar next to you and presses his belly against her back. He waves his hand (fat with U.S. dollars) in the air and makes that *tsst tsst* sound that everyone does here to get service. The bartender pours from a complicated bottle, one half dark and syrupy, the other creamy and white, and the girl— when you look close you see she must just be fourteen, her small face puttied with makeup, a patch of pimples on her chin—sucks it up through the stir straw until that dry little noise of emptiness comes from the bottom of the glass. The man waves for another, the bartender pours, the girl drinks, the man waves, the bartender pours, the girl drinks. Hatuey is fascinated with the bottle, "*¿Que bonita, eh?*" he says like he did when you were in the marketplace in Havana Vieja and he saw that contraption made out of bamboo, that thing that looked like a replica of a Chinese junk ship and was supposed to sit on a table and hold two bottles and swing back and forth if you gave it a push. You bought it for him, not wanting to judge, but nevertheless feeling more than a little let down that he chose that instead of the hand-tooled calfskin wallet or the white cotton shirt with fine stitching and shining buttons.

The thick man smells like something going bad in the sun and too much cologne. He looks over at Hatuey when the little girl finishes her third drink and gives him a wink. *"Le gusta,"* he says, but it sounds somehow German, and he paws the top of the little girl's head. Hatuey nods and smiles, showing his rotted teeth. *"Dulce,"* he says. Your stomach hurts and your head swims and you need to get away from the man and the girl, so you say to Hatuey, "Dance?" You don't realize you've spoken English until he looks at you funny. You remember the word for dance. *"Bailamos,"* you say.

"Sure," he says, the one American word he has absolutely down (only it comes out "choor"), and he takes your hand and his is warm and solid and soft and you'll follow him to the dance floor and beyond you think, and you know you're more than just a little drunk. Bodies are everywhere, moving and shaking, and it's mostly the American women with the Cubans; a few couples here and there, on honeymoon or anniversary trips; island girls with island girls dancing sexy and perfect, and you're glad you know how to move. It's something you're good at. So when Hatuey steps into your space and dips his shoulders and sways his hips just right, you move with him, and you see in his eyes how it pleases him, the way you dance, and when you get jostled by your neighbors, their high-heeled sandals heavy on their feet, their arms moving as though part of someone else's body, you don't even tip. You give in to the music, give up to the dance, and when Hatuey gets close enough to touch you, body to body this time, you let him. And you move together slow and delicious like you were made for it, and you feel the heat rise, and he lifts your hair off the back of your neck, blows cool on your burned skin and still you move and move and move. He turns his back to you, and a woman is there in front of him. He knows her, you think: she's Cuban and about his age and beautiful with a wide, full-lipped mouth and sheets of dark hair and a tiny waist, and he slides toward her and with her and at the same time reaches back for you, and you hear her say his name, "Hatuey," and she smiles over his shoulder at you, a warm, friendly, seductive smile, and you think *hot-two-way*, and it startles you, the thought, but then the girl waves to you both and dances away and it's just you and him again, and when he leans in and asks, "*¿Vamos a dormir ajuntos?*" it takes you a minute to answer because you're stuck on how the euphemism is the same as home, sleep together, and you want to be sure you know exactly what he's asking. "*¿Dormir?*" you say, and he says, "You know," and he pulls your hips against his and you feel him hard against you and so you nod.

In Centro Havana there are posters everywhere for that little boy found at sea, and while you and Hatuey walk through the close, dark streets, you imagine for a moment that you could offer yourself up in trade: your safe return to the States for the boy's safe return to Cuba. But then you remember there's no one at home who wants you back badly enough to make the trade. And it's at just this moment that Hatuey reaches for your hand, and you're so grateful for that, the way he pulls you to him, you nearly cry right there in the middle of the street. You'd like to believe it's the booze that's got you going like this, but the truth is you've danced most of it out, and you've been walking for blocks, and what you're feeling is something other than intoxicated. It's like you're fine-spun and brittle, which—you understand in this moment—is not entirely a bad thing.

When you come to the doorway that is Hatuey's, one of a dozen in a line, the whole block is blacked out. The glow of lights elsewhere rises over the low buildings like a fog. You stumble when you step inside and your heart hiccups in your chest and you remind yourself that it's adventure you are seeking, and so you trust Hatuey's lead and follow him through a room you can feel is narrow, until you reach a kitchen, and he lights a candle and pours you a rum and himself something blue that he mixes with pineapple soda. It's a tiny room, tight with furniture and appliances, a low-slung freezer, a clunky refrigerator, a dinette set made from Formica, aluminum, and vinyl. On the table there's a pile of pictures, like someone left them there in the middle of sorting, and he shows them to you: his little brother in front of a ranch house that could be in any suburb of Chicago but is in Argentina where he lives with relatives; his mother on a park bench, one hand shading her eyes from the sun; his father at about Hatuey's age, dark and thin with thick curly hair and those Cuban eyes. Hatuey kisses his fingertips and puts them on the face in each of the pictures. "*Mi papá ahora,*" he says, and he points toward the room you just passed through, "one leg, *solamente.*" He draws a line with the side of his hand beneath his own kneecap, and you understand that his father, in the other room, has had one leg amputated. You shake your head, make a sympathetic sound with your tongue on the back of your teeth. What else can you do? And you whisper, because you know now that you are not alone in this place, "*Lo siento.*" You are sorry.

"Come," Hatuey says then, and he takes your hand again and carries the candle, and you pass through that narrow room, only now in the flickering light you can make out the skinny beds on either side of it, a woman asleep in one, Hatuey's father in the other. He turns in his sleep as you pass, and you see he is a fat man, his face fleshy on the pillow, his head bald. It's hard to reconcile this aged and round one-legged person with the other man in the photo. You look at the line of Hatuey in front of you, his broad shoulders and solid ass, his long legs strong under his tight jeans. And you wonder how you will look to him once you are naked, everything forty years old and softer and lower than it once was.

His room is not really that, just a bed and a dresser on the landing at the top of the stairs. Where there might be a window, there's nothing but slats of wood and open spaces. When you sit on the edge of the bed, you fall backwards, the dilapidated box spring like a trick chair that topples the sitter. Hatuey laughs and rolls back on the bed next to you and then you are kissing, finally, and you try not to think of his brown teeth but how he tastes like scotch and pineapple. And his hair smells like smoke from the club, but his skin smells of soap, it smells powdery and fresh. He unbuttons your blouse and unzips your jeans, and you rise up so he can pull them off. "*Que bonita,*" he says and you want to believe he means you, even though he is running his finger over your black, lacy lingerie. And then he stands up and takes off his own clothes. You'd like to help, it's one of your favorite parts, but you are afraid you won't be able to get up gracefully from the sunken bed, and you figure you look better lying back and stretched out anyway, so you just watch. And his shoulders are broad, like you'd thought, but his chest is thin and boyish and hairless, which surprises you since you can still feel the burn of his stubble on your sun reddened skin. His cock is not entirely hard, and it's on the small side and uncircumcised, and it looks like a cigar, you think—a Cuban cigar. And you almost laugh but then he's on top of you and it feels warm and he helps you out of your expensive underwear and then he's inside of you and you wait for him to move like he did on the dance floor, slow and smooth and sexy. Only it's not like that. It's fast and it's over. Underneath him still, you think how when you get back home, you will remember it as long and satisfying. He rolls off you and kisses you and looks into your eyes, and his are deep and brown and you think, too, how when you get back home you will remember his eyes as Cuban and golden, like you already imagine the dark eyes of that little boy in Miami. Hatuey gathers you up in his arms and holds you and strokes your hair and whispers in that low voice how pretty you are, how he might love you, and you think how when you get back home, that will be easy to remember.

Later, when you sit in the back of the cab that takes you away from O'Hare to your place in the city, and later still, when your life alone starts to go black and white again, here's what you'll remember: you dreamed of floating on a raft shaped like a hand in the middle of the ocean somewhere between there and here, and you woke up alone in the broken-down bed. In the black there was nothing to see, but you heard from the narrow room beneath you Hatuey's voice, soft as a lover's, "*Esta bien, Papá, esta bien.*" And you heard the old man sobbing, still asleep perhaps. You'll remember how you lay there and listened ("*Shh, Papi, shh*") until the old man stopped crying and the rooms went quiet in the dark. And soon after, the sun started its slow rise. You'll remember how stripes of color, of orange, of red, of gold, came through the slats and covered the walls, the floor, the bed.

This moment, the one when dark turns to light, is what you'll carry away with you back to your too-big apartment in the city. This. This is what you'll remember most of all.

I AM NOT AFRAID

No woman deserves to be treated this way — none of us deserves this kind of abuse.

—MICHELLE OBAMA

I overheard a friend recently say that every woman is afraid every day.

I am not afraid.

Despite living in Chicago, a city that a presidential candidate would have us believe is as dangerous as Baghdad. Despite having my ass grabbed in a crowded museum in this same city when I was on a field trip when I was twelve. Despite my looking behind me into the crowd of faces (all kids, all around my age, boys and girls, some I knew, some I did not) and meeting no eyes, seeing no sympathy. Despite my turning back (*maybe I imagined it*) to the exhibit, a slice of a human embryo pressed between panes of glass, and again having my ass grabbed. Despite hearing the snickers behind me.

I am not afraid.

Despite having a man come into the Iowa gas station in a safe city where I worked a register during my twenties, come in a few times a week during the evening rush and go into the bathroom, come out with his zipper down and his dick visible, right in my line of sight because that is where he held out his hand to me with his money for the gas he had pumped, for the six pack he had grabbed from the cooler, right there at open-zippered dick level, and the line behind him was long and shuffling, eager to get home to dinner, to the nightly news, to *Jeopardy*, and it took me a few times of the same damn thing to understand that this was not an accident. This was not an accident.

And to accuse, no matter who it is, a man or a woman, without evidence is damaging and unfair.
                                                                    –MELANIA TRUMP

Still, I am not afraid.

Despite having had a man lure me into Grant Park in this most dangerous city when I was thirteen. Lure me with the promise of five bucks just to listen to him tell a little joke. Despite the joke not being a joke at all, but a stream of filthy, dirty things that he spit out of his mouth while he pulled his dick out and started jacking off, and, like I've said I was thirteen, right? Remember? And what could I do? And what could I do? I said I would go with him. I wanted five dollars. And he finished and I followed him out of the park to a bank where he said he was going to get five dollars; he was going to give me ten I was so nice. And I stood outside the bank thinking I had done something worth at least ten bucks, and feeling a little sick with that, a little sad, and the motherfucker never came out. I don't know where he went, where he disappeared to, but I didn't see him again. Not that day. But another and another, and I do still, see him everywhere, on the street, on the El, in Grant Park, even though I don't really see him at all.

How about a little hug for the Bushy?

–BILLY BUSH

I am not afraid.

Despite having my boobs grabbed while I had my hands up over my head holding a tray of corned-beef sandwiches that I was selling in a packed bar on Division Street in this dangerous city on Saint Patrick's Day when I was twenty-two.

Despite having one of my brother's friends show up at our house when I was nine and home alone, sick from school. My brother's friend who I had always had a crush on. A teenager. Show up at the house when I was home sick from school—how did he know? And make me a hot rum toddy (because it would make my throat less sore) and climb under the covers with me, which I liked. And cuddle me. Which I liked. And put his fingers inside me. Which I did not like.

Wow! Just think—in a couple of years, I'll be dating you.

–DONALD TRUMP

I am not afraid.

Despite having been slipped a valium in my drink at a club by a man I was seeing when I was twenty-one and living in a small, safe city in Iowa, a man who was staying with me and who I was having sex with already, and had intended to have sex with again that night when we got back to my house after the club, so why did he think he needed to drug me? (I never did ask him. *Why didn't I ask him?*)

Despite (also in Iowa, in a safe, small city) once having sex with a man on our first (and only) date who I didn't want to have sex with (sometimes I did on the first date, not with him, but with others I liked better, with others I wanted to have sex with, my choice) but who would not leave me alone and would not go home until I did, and I did, because it was easier to say yes than to say no (you know what I mean, you know it) and my brother was asleep in the next room, our housemate was asleep in another room close by, and I was embarrassed to be half-naked on the couch of my own living room, exposed, (I would not invite him into my bedroom, into my bed, he would not get that from me,) and I just wanted this guy gone. Here, you can have this. Just this. Now go.

Despite having had to resist a guy I knew in college in safe Iowa who, when we sat next to one another in the grass in the dark, a little drunk, a Friday night, finals over, when we kissed, he thought that meant we would fuck, and it did not mean — to my mind — that we would fuck, and I said no. No. No. But the only way I could get him to stop trying to push me down, trying to open my blouse, pull down my jeans, was to promise him we would do this later, not that night, but another, I promise. We never did, and I don't know why, but it never came up again (pun unintended, but hey, laugh, if you like, we all need to laugh sometimes) even though our paths crossed often. It was a very small school.

These allegations are decades old. If somebody actually did that...any reasonable woman would have come forward and said something at the time.

–A.J. DELGADO

I am not afraid.

Despite having been trapped by — not a co-worker, but a very rich friend of my boss when I worked on the trading floor of the Chicago Mercantile Exchange — in an empty hallway where he held me and started kissing me and had a look in his eyes I hadn't seen from him before; he was a nice guy, a funny guy. An angry look. A hateful one. I thought at the time that it may have been because he had lost a lot of money in trades that day, and had recently broken up with his longtime girlfriend (she didn't want to marry him), and his dog had died just a few days before. And why the fuck am I making excuses for him anyway?

We accepted it for years...We were taught it was our fault.
                                                                    –JESSICA LEEDS

I am not afraid.

Despite this. All this. And now I am in my sixth decade (*Believe me, she would not be my first choice.* –Donald Trump) and perhaps I have less to fear, perhaps I have more. But I am not afraid.

You can do anything...Grab them by the pussy. You can do anything.
                                                                    –DONALD TRUMP

I pledge to every citizen of our lands [sic] that I will be the president for the American people.
                                                    –PRESIDENT ELECT DONALD TRUMP

I am not afraid.
    I am not.
    Afraid.

THERE IS A LIGHT THAT NEVER GOES OUT
(with apologies and appreciation to Morrissey)

My father died, as I have said, when I was fifteen years old; I was still a virgin. I know what you are thinking: non sequitur. What does one thing have to do with the other? I know what I am thinking: everything. When I was fifteen I hung out with a fast crowd. (Do people still say that? Fast. As in wild. As in "She was fast." As in sexually active.) There were only two of us who had not yet gone all the way, or the euphemism our gang liked to use — who knows why? We thought it was cute, clever, cryptic (as if) — only two of us had not yet "fallen off the cherry tree." Me — as I've said — and my best friend, Helen.

Not like there hadn't been ample opportunity. Make-out parties in my other friend Jane's finished basement where we'd turn out the lights and find corners and cubbyholes away from one another but in pairs, couples, boy/girl because those who were more inclined toward boy/boy or girl/girl hadn't admitted it yet. Early seventies. So we'd braid together in the powder room, the utility room, on the couch (usually Jane got the couch, because it was her basement after all), behind the wet bar, under the pool table. Or we'd pair up and sneak into the backseats of our neighbors' cars, left unlocked and parked on the streets, or — if our boyfriends were older — in the backseats of their cars in a forest preserve parking lot, windows clouded over with the heat of our want. Or we'd twine our legs over legs in the grass, stretched out under the stars on a summer night in a field behind the junior high. And there was babysitting: kids asleep and parents away and nothing but time and autonomy and forgotten homework assignments piled on the kitchen table.

So, yeah, I didn't have to be a virgin when my dad died. But I was. The kissing was fun. The groping. The rubbing. I liked all that. But I guess I just didn't care enough to fall (jump?) off the cherry tree. Didn't care enough about the boy(s), about the act, about the admittance into the club of nonvirgins.

Sidebar: for a long while, years, decades, I measured the time passed since my father's death and how long since I had been a virgin in the same equation. I don't anymore, but for the record, as I write this, it has been forty years since I last saw my dad, and just a little shy of that since I last saw my virginity. That makes me fifty-five. And coincidentally, or maybe not so, maybe this is why I have been thinking about death and sex (even more than usual) lately, why my mind trips around these things, memories and wonders and words, my dad was fifty-five when he died.

So once my dad died, I made it my mission to get laid, and also to do it before Helen did; I didn't want to be the last of my friends to cross the line. I'll spare you most of the details but these: a slightly older guy named Nick I met at the Holiday, a dark, cavernous disco on Elston that let minors onto the dance floor, but not into the bar; an immigrant from a country we used to call Yugoslavia; busboy by trade; backseat of a Ford; the Sunset drive-in theater on McCormick. November. My dad died in October. Did I love him? Nick, I mean, because yes, I loved my father. Nick? Absolutely not. In fact, that was essential to me, to not love the first man I slept with. Because if things didn't work out, I did not want to be devastated by the loss. By another loss. He was cute, though, Nick was, long hair and big brown eyes. And when it was over, I was glad to know that if I were to suddenly, unexpectedly, die — say of a massive heart attack while I was shopping for groceries, like my father did — at least I would not die a virgin. I would not miss out on this big, important thing.

Death. Sex.

On the day of my first marriage, while my about-to-be-husband and I stood on a beach in the Bahamas, a planned elopement with a few strangers in attendance and the mayor of the island officiating and a flea-bitten dog at our feet, my mother, back home in Chicago on a cold March day was diagnosed with a bit of breast cancer. I say bit because that's what it was, just a bit that they cut out of her breast, leaving a bite-sized crescent in the lump's wake; they gave her pills and sent her home. The cancer went away. My first marriage did, too.

Marriage. Illness.

On the day of my last wedding ("last" not just because it was the most recent, but also the one I intend to be my last, we are together still, silly and kissy-faced and hand-holding and — forgive me this word — partners after more than a decade and no end — thankfully — in sight) my mother was dying from lung cancer. In our wedding photos, taken here in Chicago, our good friends and family in the frames with us celebrating our union, my mother looks happy and a little chubby-cheeked from the chemo and the steroids, knowing, like we all did, that her end was near, but she was here now, goddamnit, in her pretty lavender mother-of-the-bride dress and perfect wig and she was proud and loving and hanging on for one last party.

Marriage. Death. Love.

You're thinking: morbid. I'm thinking: not at all. Exquisite. These things, these wonderful (full of wonder) and awful (full of awe) things—death, sex, marriage, illness, love—are beautifully, intricately entwined. *La petit morte*, the little death, the French call an orgasm. A sort of transcendence. Highpoints in the splendid whole of life. These last weeks—since my fifty-fifth birthday—I've been carrying a Smiths song around in my head, its title the title of this piece. Morrissey imploring a friend to take him out where there's music and people young and alive. The song is darkness and light and love; it is wonderful and awful: "and if a double-decker bus crashes into us," and the rest of that verse, "to die by your side" and so on. It's a good thing.

Love. Death.

Did you know that February 14, Saint Valentine's Day, is thought to be the anniversary of Saint Valentine's death? And that he was tortured before he died (on February 14) in prison? That he was imprisoned for secretly marrying couples, defying an order by the emperor Claudius? Love, death, pain, torture, marriage. Celebration.

Will you be my Valentine? Will you marry me? Will you die for me?

These are the things I think about forty years after I lost my virginity in the arms of a Yugoslavian busboy in the backseat of a Ford on a warm November night at the drive-in. What movie? I can't remember. It hurt a little, I remember that. Like love does sometimes. Like sex can. Like grief. Forty years after I called my friend Helen when I got home that night and told her: "I win." Twelve years since I told this husband I do, I will, in a tiny chapel with a rose garden named for Shakespeare; with our mothers, our brothers, our friends and a Buddhist monk in attendance. Twelve years since my mom died three months after this last wedding, opening her eyes one final time to see me there next to her in a hospital bed set up in her living room, during the dark of night when others elsewhere slept and whispered and read and made love in their own beds. To die by your side, the song goes. Sex. Love. Death. The things I think about at the start of my fifty-fifth year. Will I live longer than my dad? Can I make it to my mom's age when she passed? Seventy-eight. That's a lot of years yet. And if things go my way, a lot more sex yet. More love. More of this long-living marriage I'm in.

Death and sex and marriage and illness and marriage and death and love. Let's face it, that's about all there is, and some of us don't even get that much. Some of us might get just a couple of these things. We all get at least one. For the rest of us though, you know, this fast crowd I hang with, we just might get it all. I'm thinking of Morrissey again on the eve of Saint Valentine's Day in my fifty-fifth year as I look ahead, as I look behind. That song, those words about love and death. About good stuff and bad. "Well," he sings, and here's the good part, "the pleasure, the privilege, is mine."

And on this snowy February evening while teenagers cloud the windows of cars and pair off in the corners of basements somewhere, everywhere, that is precisely what I have been thinking. The pleasure, the privilege, is mine.

NOURISHMENT
In Three Parts

1
A Girl Scout Saved My Life

It's cold and flu season. Is that really a season or just a marketing ploy for advertisers? "This cold and flu season, be prepared. Stock up on Stoppacough. Guaranteed to stop *your* cough." And a picture (moving or still, depending on budget) of a mother and a child, a girl, say, with her baby blond hair tangled just a little on the crown of her head where her mother pets her, mother at daughter's side on the pink-quilted bed, holding the girl, pink-cheeked (must be the fever), the girl holding a stuffed animal, a bunny maybe, or a puppy (no bear, too cliché) and she's smiling weakly, her coughing stopped at least for this moment, a prominent product placement bedside, the lamp (it is dim in the room, twilight or early morning beyond the frilly curtains) shining brightly on the multi-colored label on a bottle of something liquid and orange: STOPPACOUGH!

But I digress. I find myself doing that lately, and not just now, and not just because I am sick. We've had an election recently, and it has caused my mind to—well, wander is not the exact word here—caused my mind to spin. My thoughts, like our future, are ajumble.

Start again: It is cold and flu season and I have a cold.

Or maybe the flu. Coughing ridiculously, like bad acting in a hospital scene on a daytime soap opera. Snorting. Blowing my nose. My skin is either slick with feverish sweat or goosebumped from the waves of the chills that wash over me. And I remember the times I have been as discomforted by the cold or flu before. Last spring, in a hotel room in northern Michigan when a snowstorm grounded me and I went through a dozen boxes of crap, sandpapery, industrial tissue. For three days, the maids left replacement boxes outside my door, and I picked them up when I put the tied-tight, used tissue filled plastic bin liners out for them to throw away.

When I was twenty and a bartender in Iowa and at the end of my night shift, two in the morning (*Last call!* We used to yell at closing time. *You don't have to go home, but you can't stay here!*) and I lay down in a booth that smelled like stale beer and burnt popcorn and unclean jeans, and shook and ached and fell asleep until the next day, morning light, when the day staff came in and turned on the lights and started the jukebox (...*Lucille, four hungry...*) and looked genuinely frightened when I sat up then, disoriented and ugly, my eyes fiery with fever, my nose crusted and sleep-drool dried over my cheeks and chin.

When I arrived in Prague to teach in 2009, when we had a new president and so much hope. When Michael Jackson had just died and my students were young and healthy and energetic and I spent the first two days of the term under a blanket on the couch of my temporary suite, listening to them calling to one another on the other side of my door, to their footfalls up and down the stairs, to their voices in the street below my window.

And that time when I was twenty-four or -five and

living in a high-rise on the edge of Chicago's Gold Coast with floor-to-ceiling windows that overlooked the tracks of the Brown Line (only then we called it the Ravenswood) and beyond that, Cabrini Green, one of Chicago's notoriously bad experiments in high-rise project ghettoization. Early eighties. My windows opened on a slant at the bottom of them, shin level, a space just big enough to let air in, but small enough to keep a body from falling out. Efficient, double-paned, which was good because there was a bullet hole in the outer pane of one of them. Don't ask.

But the flu, the flu. I was so fevered and weak, I hadn't been to work in days. (Office manager of a Division Street nightclub-restaurant.) I lay in my bed trembling, skin stinging, coughing, moaning. I became addicted to *Sally Jessy Raphael* (Google it.) I hurt so bad — my throat, my joints, my skin, my head, my ribs from coughing — I wasn't even hungry. Until, that is, days in and on the mend, I was.

In the early eighties — truth even now — I was not much of a cook. I worked in a restaurant (as I've said) where my meals were free. I was a half-block from a 7-Eleven, two blocks from Jewel. Finding a meal, pretty much anytime of the day or night, was never an issue. Money and convenience, I — unlike some (my brother then and now gets many of his meals at soup kitchens; he stocks his cabinets with canned goods from food pantries. He has a job, but it's part-time and pays all right but not enough to live well in this city, even with his supplemental disability income) — had both. I could afford food.

But I didn't have any. I rarely did. A jar of peanut butter sometimes, because I got a craving and it tastes so good by the spoonful. A chocolate chip muffin, one of two, softball-sized muffins sold in pairs in plastic cartons from Jewel (or as we say in Chicagoese, *The* Jewel.) Pepsis. That's as stocked as my larders ever got.

And on the third or fourth day of this body-breaking flu I had, there was nothing left. Nothing. I drank water by the gallons, and my stomach gurgled with it.

Here is a little something about me. I am loath to ask for help. Pretty much all the time. "Need help carrying those groceries? That suitcase? Those moving boxes? That couch?" Nope. Nope. Nope. Nope. Thanks, though. I got it.

A normal person—one who understands that being alive pretty much means being part of something, a community, say, or a family—would, in my flu-weakened, near-starved state, have called a friend, a family member and asked: "Hey, would you mind picking me up a can of soup? Maybe some orange juice? A loaf of bread?" And the friend or family member would have said, "Sure! Anything else? Maybe a few frozen Swanson dinners? Do you need fruit?"

Not me.

Believe me when I tell you that during that particular bout of the flu, I tried to tend to myself. I tried to fend for myself. I dragged (a precise verb here, picture Neanderthal crawling from the cave) myself out of my sick-stinking bed and turned on the shower. I sat on the lid of the toilet until I gathered enough strength to climb over the side of the tub and under the stream. When I tried to wash my hair (days of sweat mixed with eighties mousse and hair-helmet-spray) the effort of lifting my arms up nearly made me pass out. I sat in the bottom of the tub and let the water rain down on me. I ran the soap over my body parts in slow, inch-by-inch increments, parceling out my energy until, twenty to twenty-five minutes later, the water ran cold and I was more or less clean.

And then I dragged myself back to my filthy bed and squirmed under the covers. There was no way I was going to be able to leave my apartment to get food. I had no cash, and in those days, for pizza or Chinese delivery, you had to have cash. My hair seeped shower water into my pillowcase, and I was glad to be able to lie down again. I felt lucky (or perhaps unlucky) just to be alive.

I woke up to a knock on my door. Odd, because I was on the sixteenth floor of a secure building with a doorman. People had to be announced, approved, buzzed up. You couldn't just walk in. You couldn't get to my sixteenth-floor door from the outside without my knowing, without my permission.

"Hello?" I called as best I could from my bed. I would have been able to see who it was through the peephole, but there was no way I could get to the peephole. It wasn't a large apartment, two rooms and a small bath, a tiny wedge of a kitchen. I could see the front door from my bed. I could see the shadows beneath it breaking up the perpetual light of the common hallway.

Knock knock. (Again.)

"Hello?" (Again.)

"Girl Scout cookies," a little voice called back.

"Excuse me?" I called in return. An auditory hallucination, surely.

A little louder: "Girl Scout cookies. I have your order. Girl Scout cookies."

Hallelujah! Praise be! Thank you, Juliette Gordon Low, Girl Scout founder, lifesaver, matron saint of small girls and flu-stricken, twenty-something women!

My hunger propelled me then — a flight response, or a fight one, I always get those confused — and I was at the door opening it widely enough to grab the boxes (Thin Mints, Tagalongs, Samoas) from the pink hands of the startled girl who lived in my building, down the hall, whose mother stood back against a wall, watching, because of course she would not be foolish enough to let her child knock on the apartment doors of her neighbors by herself, security building or no.

"Sorry," I said. "Sick," I said. "Thanks," I said. I pushed the door closed between us. I leaned against the cool fireproof material of it and slid down to the carpet. I opened the Thin Mints. Thin Mints! Even now I can taste the relief of them — can't you? Chocolate and cool, crunchy freshness, sweet, sweet sustenance. I pulled one, then another, then another from the plastic sleeve. I licked the melted goodness from my fingertips.

I ate. I lived. A Girl Scout saved my life. Thin Mints on the carpet: rarely, rarely, has anything ever tasted so good.

2

BBQ From The IC

When I was thirteen, I would go to work with my dad in the Loop and do his filing and phone answering. I felt like a grown-up. Lunchtimes he would send me out to the Illinois Central Railroad Station where there was a little barbecue stand. I got barbecued chicken, and for many, many years after that, if anyone asked what my favorite food was, I'd answer: "barbecued chicken." Dad worked in one of the last buildings in the city that had elevator operators, and when I'd get in the elevator car with my bag of barbecue, the man at the controls always sniffed the air and made jokes about how hungry he was.

Can I describe to you what it was like sitting across from my dad at his desk, our fingers greasy with BBQ sauce and salty from French fries, talking about — what? I can't remember. But I remember those lunches, and how since then, very few meals have ever been as satisfying.

3
Montejaque 2009

The handwritten trail map we'd found in a book on a shelf in our rented house warned us of "deadly sharp cacti" and it was right. It promised an easy pass across the ridge, but it was wrong. We moved slowly over jagged rocks and slick drops, our feet sideways and slipping. The map didn't mention the goat farm with the farmer smoking and leaning on the tilted gate, watching our approach, knowing his way was the only way. "*Permiso*," we begged, and he put the cigarette between his teeth, pulled back the gate, let us pass, mud up to our ankles. The goats stared, jaws moving. We found the chapel, what we'd set out for, small and white on a mountainside. We stopped, sat in the cool of it on wooden benches worn curved by more than a century of sitting.

I was about to turn fifty, we had a new president, an elegant man, just days away from his inauguration. People celebrated his election in Grant Park across from where my office is, under my window high up in a building that overlooks that park and the lake beyond. I was in England when he was elected, but I woke up when my husband Philip called me, when he told me the news. I could hear in Philip's voice what I knew he could hear in mine. Awe. Wonder. Delight. That was what I knew, but among the things I didn't know were still ahead of me were these: my first half-marathon; the death of my closest brother while I sat at his side in a ritzy Chicago hospital and held his hand; the publication of my first book; a hysterectomy; my second half-marathon. Two terms of a president we were eager to elect, and would miss when he was gone.

Half a century. Half-marathons. Half-way on our hike.

The road down from the chapel was steep; I steadied myself on the shoulders of my husband, steps ahead of me, below me. At the bottom of the hill, back in the whitewashed village, we found a *taverna* and drank cold beer and ate potato chips and *bocadillos*, the bread still warm from the oven. We dabbed our cactus scrapes with paper napkins dipped in glasses of ice water.

We spread the map between us and tried to figure out where we'd gone wrong, where we'd veered off-course. The inked lines moved easily over the worn creases where the page had been folded and folded again. There was nothing besides those lines or between them. No slick rocks, no muddy farm, no chewing, gaping goats.

There's a metaphor here, about winding paths, about things in the road, about not knowing what's ahead, about finding our way. Now, on the eve of our next president as I write this, a man who does not inspire delight or awe in me, and only wonder in scary, what's-next sort of ways, I am uncertain how we got here, how we got so very, very lost. But back in Montejaque it was a day before my fiftieth birthday, two years before my book launch, a year before my brother's death, and months and years before the rest of it, before now. And then, I wasn't interested in metaphors. I could feel the hike in my thighs. We ordered more food, more beer. Out in the courtyard, we could see through the window, a man cleaned a cage filled with chirping parakeets. Potato chips from a plastic bag. Cold beer. Warm bread.

Nourishment.

WRITING, WONDER, LONELINESS, AND PLACE

A STORIED LIFE

I sit with my first husband at a restaurant in Chicago's Lakeview, and across the way near a large, haunting, abstract painting on a brick-face wall, another couple lean in toward one another, then away. The man leaves his hand on the table between them, palm up; the woman pulls her shoulders back and crosses her arms over her chest. She is weeping.

I lived in a house in a small subdivision between two lakes in Iowa and the wife of the couple next door was badly scarred. A deep caving in of flesh was where bone and muscle should have been, but wasn't. I found out later that her husband shot half of her face off. A hunting accident. They gave up hunting. She stopped eating meat.

On a huge Ferris wheel that towers over Navy Pier and looks out onto the great lake—one with swinging cages instead of bench seats—I watch as a father lets his little boy, an infant, crawl around the floor of the ride, putting his head against the bars that are supposed to keep us safe.

When I worked on the trading floor of the Chicago Mercantile Exchange, I knew twin brothers who—in their forties, perhaps fifties—still dressed alike and lived together. They were each single, never married. One was the nice one. One was not.

In my teens I babysat in the well-heeled northern suburbs for a girl with Down's syndrome. She was younger than me, but actually quite a bit larger, heavier. One afternoon while she settled in for a nap, I dozed on a couch in the den. I woke up when the girl was on top of me, hitting me.

Friends tell me stories: there's a woman with a double mastectomy and a man working in her house; a mother tried to give up eating in order to find enlightenment; a woman suspected her husband of cheating only to find out he was distracted by his serious (and secret) illness. I listen carefully and store it all away, just in case. One writer friend knows what I am up to, and so she prefaces her stories—the really good ones—with *Now, you can't have this one; this one is mine.*

They are all ordinary moments from my ordinary life, but ones that stay with me, draw me to them and through them in search of narrative. I gather these instances, never quite sure when they will present themselves to me, unbidden at times, or at others, dragged out from the murky shadows of memory. I sit in a chair near a window that overlooks the city side street, my pen and journal in hand or my fingers on a keyboard, and scan through those things I have witnessed, I've been told, I've noted, and I wonder about still—days, years, sometimes decades after this happened, after that occurred.

Here—in each day I make my way through—is where story lives. The couple pulling apart at the table, the scarred wife, the endangered child, the odd twins, the big girl and her babysitter, the man in the house, the longing mother, and the distracted husband each have found a home in my first book of stories. They are no longer the people I saw or was told about, they are no longer the people I knew in real life. They have become others, characters created who populate the pages of the tales I've imagined in these new lives I've discovered.

It is this, this moving from watching, gathering, storing away, to writing it down that changes things. What was real, what really happened, no longer matters, at least not to me. It is an interesting tension, this pull between observation and imagination, this balance of seeing it happen and making it happen. This place that is settled somewhere between what is real and what is imagined is where I come to do my work; this is where I live my storied life.

FIVE BARS, TWO TAVERNS, TWO TAPS
Chicago, 1999

North of Wrigleyville, there's a bar called Joy-Blue. It's cozy and hip, with low sofas and real artwork. Sort of a coffeehouse serving designer martinis. It used to be Austin City Limits, the kind of tavern my dad took me to when I was a kid, where I'd play the jukebox and sit on a vinyl barstool and drink Squirts. A dark, smoky, sticky-floored place that served Old Style on tap and Schlitz in a bottle—and the really good stuff was Wild Turkey. A place filled with working folks in uniforms or shirtsleeves, stopping by for a quick one before they'd head on home. That's the kind of bar Austin City Limits was. Blue-collar, mostly, a little grubby, but as comfortable and familiar as a pair of old jeans. Digger, one of the regulars, worked at Graceland cemetery down the street (so he said). He would tell ghost stories for a shot of whiskey. But that was then. Joy-Blue is now.

I stand near the bar with a sweating, ice-cold bottle of imported beer in my hand. Nearly everyone else has huge, funny-colored martinis in theirs. It's a promotional thing—flavored martinis on special—and the regulars (my neighbors who are young and professional and live in the brand new condo buildings with their babies and dogs) drink it up. There's no denying they are working folks too, only I don't imagine any of them digs graves for a living. New baby stories take the place of old ghost stories, but some topics—whether you're sipping a chocolate martini or slugging a Schlitz—never change: the Bulls (before and after Michael Jordan), the Cubs, the CTA, the mayor.

The talk at Toons, a bar down the block, is real estate. "See the new buildings?" the bartender asks as he slides me a glass of beer. How could I not? They're going up on both sides of the bar: on one side a narrow tract of condos that sell for around $300,000 (1999, remember), on the other side "Luxury Townhomes" that start at nearly half a million. I drink my beer and take in Toons. It smells of booze, like a good bar should, and caters to a young, jeans-and-T-shirt crowd. Singles, mostly, from the apartments in the neighborhood, and some older men in flannel shirts who like a cold drink, a good game of pool, someone to talk to. The drink of choice here is beer. I can't help but wonder, though, if as the new buildings around Toons go up, the martini consumption will too.

Down the street there's more construction and new restaurants and specialty stores filled with antiques and art and kiddy toys made for a safe planet and slices of carrot cake that cost at least three bucks. And more places to drink. The neighborhood has five bars, two taverns, two taps. The distinction between bar and tavern, as far as I can tell, is in name only. There's the Launder Bar (have a beer while your clothes spin) and the Schoolyard Tavern. The Schoolyard's not like the dark, wood-paneled taverns I used to know; it's bright and clubby like a college bar. University affiliations mark sweatshirts and ball caps, and the average customer is maybe twenty-two.

The taps are the old places. One is nameless—the

Words *On Tap* on a lighted sign. It's been here forever. The customers are old-timers, too. Many of them grew up here, lived as kids in the houses they own now. They talk about when they went to the elementary school down the road, when they played basketball in the park. As I walk into On Tap, they eye me closely. To them, I'm one of the newcomers, just seven years in the neighborhood. To me, though, this place is like the tavern I grew up in. "A beer," I say, and since there aren't many choices, I take whatever is cold and wet and tasty on tap.

The other one, Lange's, displays signs inviting the neighborhood in to watch Sunday football. Not many of the condo owners go there. Mostly, it's just Lange's regulars: men whose hard work shows in the muscles of their arms, whose love of libation shows in their rounded bellies; black-haired women dressed in fuzzy, glittering, "dressy" sweaters. They drink beer, listen to oldies on the jukebox and are likely to get a good laugh out of a bad joke. The young customers are punkish, pierced and tattooed. Beer drinkers, too, who wouldn't be caught dead with a blue martini in a launder or fraternity or coffeehouse bar. They talk about the art movie playing close by at the Music Box, and they, too, listen to the oldies.

On a crisp evening, I walk down the street past the side-walk tables most of the joints keep up late into fall. Everyone's out: the punks, the singles, the young marrieds with their kids and dogs, the old-timers. While I wait for a table at one of the restaurants, I see an elderly guy at the bar, alone and out of place in jeans and a Western-style shirt. He and the bartender share a language of hand signals that keeps the guy's glass filled with beer. A couple in expensive suits walk in and they sit next to the guy. That's the neighborhood for you, I'm thinking: shiny, affluent, new against slightly-out-of-place old. And then the woman deliberately bumps shoulders with the old guy. He looks up from his beer. His face spreads wide with a smile.

"Howzit going?" the old man says.

"Good," the woman replies.

"Where you been?" the old man asks.

"We took a trip," she says, and catches the eye of the bartender, draws a circle with her finger in the air. The bartender serves a round for the three of them. "Europe," her partner says.

"Haven't been there since the war," the old man says. "Bet it's changed some. Got pictures?"

And then my table's ready and the waiter's there, waiting. "A beer," I say.

I hear the old man at the bar laugh and I see the young woman put a hand on his arm. And I think about how, though the neighborhood continues to change, some things stay the same. Like this: The old man at the bar raises his glass, the young woman clinks hers to his. They toast. They drink. They talk.

WE ARE ALL JUST STUPID PEOPLE

"**Y**our characters are so stupid," the woman said. She sat at the other end of the table, directly across from me. It was a bright blue winter day, and the book club met high over the city, with views of season-bare Millennium Park and of the great frozen lake and of snow piles going gray in the gutters. "I felt like slapping some of them!"

Okay, maybe this isn't exactly what she said, this bit about my stupid characters, but it was something like that. (She did say the slapping part, though.) I'd been invited to speak with the book club about my first book, a collection of short stories, and I was, as I always am by these invitations, honored. I relish the opportunity to speak with readers; I've visited book clubs in living rooms and restaurants, shared brunch and dinner and coffee and drinks with avid and curious readers of all ages; I've read to them, talked with them, answered questions, filled them in on what parts of the book are "true" and what parts aren't. (Yes, I knew identical twin brothers who dressed alike into their forties; no, they never murdered anyone that I know of. Yes, I hit a deer once with my car; yes, I had a neighbor whose husband shot half her face off; no, I haven't had a mastectomy; yes, I have been unfaithful; no, I was never part of a cult.)

Perhaps you might discern from the parentheticals above that the book is not a particularly light read. There aren't a lot of happy endings (although some I'd call bittersweet) and my characters get into trouble — often of their own making. And this book-club lady in front of me (as well as a number of the other readers around the table) did not like that.

"Why didn't he do something?"

"Why didn't they stop him?"

"Why didn't she get out of there?"

And then what, I wish I would have asked. *Where's the story in that?*

Imagine *The Grapes of Wrath* if the Joads had turned back, got out of there, gave up their journey. The family, Steinbeck's creation, shrinks by death and desertion, and yet they plod on. We, as readers, root for them, even though we are fairly certain that things will not turn out well. No happy endings here. And literature is all the better for it.

The writer Richard Bausch once said in an interview, "…the thing that produces change is trouble. Even the happiest event is fraught with it, because we all know that the one promise life always keeps is suffering. Loss. Confusion. Grief. And writing about all those things matters because the subjects themselves matter." He said as well, "…I'm always interested in the hurt people carry around."

Me too.

I remember when I first read Raymond Carver. I came to him late-ish in life, like I did the active pursuit of writing. I'd dropped out of college and wasted time, bartending and managing a gas station, and finally spending a chunk of my twenties and thirties working in the financial markets in Chicago. And it was on a lunch break that I wandered into a bookstore (trying to get as far away from the noise of the open outcry on the trading floor as I could) and found *What We Talk About When We Talk About Love*. I'd been a big reader as a kid, as a teenager. But it had been a long, long time (for some reason) since I'd read much of anything besides the daily paper and my horoscope. This collection of stories was a slim one, and, having fallen out of the practice of reading, I found its skinniness appealing. I stood in an aisle among fiction titles and other lunchtime browsers and read "Popular Mechanics," the very short story about a couple who divide their things as they pull their marriage (and their baby, the reader comes to understand) apart.

"Holy sh…" I whispered to myself at the brief and stunning story. I turned the pages, looking for another — well — gut punch, I guess.

Still standing, I read "The Bath."

"You can do that?" I don't know if I said this out loud, but whenever I think about that day in the bookstore decades ago (and I think about it often), I hear those words in my head. "You can do that?"

What I meant: you can write a story that ends in such a tragic and bleak way that it hurts like looking at something too shiny, too beautiful, and still make your reader come back for more? My reading history had held mostly popular fiction, the books my girlfriends shared full of wish fulfilment and happy endings, or in school, stories with lessons, morals. I think it was all of that goodness, happiness, and lesson teaching that drove me away from reading in the first place. Finding a happy ending or moral in books and movies is easy, like microwaving a Hot Pocket for lunch. Happy, moralistic endings are sweet and comforting but ultimately without much nourishment and far from satisfying. I had grown tired of Hot Pockets.

The book club high above the city wanted (as some book clubs do) happy endings; not even the endings of my stories that I consider to be hopeful and bittersweet, nor the moments inside the stories that I mean to provide grace, caring, human connection, were enough for them. I told them I don't often do happy endings, and they were disappointed. I was disappointed, too, that they would rather leave the pages of a book happy than curious and longing. If everyone lives happily ever after, then we don't need to wonder about them anymore, do we? I passed up striving for the happy ending in order to try to create something that might be beautiful and moving, that might make me ache a little. For me as a writer, as a reader, reaching an ending where I find beauty and where I am moved, even if it's a sad ending, makes me happy. But I didn't tell them that, I hadn't yet put it into words for myself. Even so, I don't think it would have mattered that winter day.

"I was even starting to worry about you," the woman at the other end of the table said (like I lacked some sort of moral fiber), conflating the sorry parts of my characters' lives with my own.

I have a good and happy life. I do. A solid job. A caring husband. Cats and travel and friends. And yet, some of the most remarkable moments that I carry with me, that I have been exceptionally moved by, changed by, stunned by, are these: the unexpected news of the death of my father when I was fifteen and the way one of my brothers sunk to the floor in grief and despair; my nephew, afraid of me for some reason on a sunny afternoon, dashing across a wet patio and slipping, scraping his knees and hands and crying in embarrassment and pain; a grade school guidance counselor dabbing her own eyes as she told me of my brother's attempt at suicide; my mother dying in the middle of the night while I held her; coming home to an empty apartment after my first husband moved out, the hollow sound that came from the lock as I turned it.

These are the moments I want to tell, to write, the ones that leave me a little raw, that hold love and loneliness and memory and pain and suffering and survival. "Beauty is created out of the labor of human hands and minds. It is to be found, precarious, at some tense edge where symmetry and asymmetry, simplicity and complexity, order and chaos, contend," the chemist and poet Roald Hoffman wrote.

"Your characters are so stupid," the book-club lady — with the lake sparkling coldly beyond the window behind her — said. Or something like that. And what I now wish I had said: "Yes, yes they are. And so are you. And so am I." Because let's face it, we are all just stupid people, carrying our hurt around. Even the smartest among us make mistakes, take the wrong turn, sit when we should stand up, drop the thing we should catch. We are fallible and we are resilient. James Salter, the novelist, said: "I deem as heroic those who have the harder task, face it unflinchingly and live." Live, Salter said, not triumph.

And happy endings or no, this is what I want. I want my characters, these stupid people, to face it (whatever it is) unflinchingly, I want them to carry their hurt around, I want them to stand at the tense edge where order and chaos contend. And most of all, I want my characters, my stupid characters, to live.

YOUR COMFORTABLE SHOPPING

I stand in line at Albert, a Prague supermarket where I've just spent half an hour wandering the aisles looking for something familiar. Peanut butter. Thousand Island dressing. I cannot read the aisle markers that are, of course, in Czech. All I want, really, is water (*voda*), and maybe some apricots (*meruňky*), and some cheese (*sýr*). Bread (*chléb*). I squeeze past the Czechs doing their Saturday shopping, unable to make my mouth parcel out *s dovolením* (excuse me.) It doesn't really matter anyway. No one says that here. No one talks all that much in public, in that polite-society way we North Americans, we midwesterners especially, do. They walk in front of one another, bump into each other, step on one another's heels without so much as a *promiňte* (forgive me). They pass one another on the street, meet eyes, and look away. No smile, no *dobrý den* (good day). And here, in this city of history and culture and more than one million residents, I pine for these small moments of human contact, of connection.

I'm in Prague during the summer of 2004 with a small group of students from Columbia College Chicago where I teach creative writing, and we are staying in a working-class neighborhood many tram stops away from the more popular Old Town Square. Good, I think, wanting not to feel like a tourist. At best, I'd like to be considered a local, someone who belongs in a certain place; at worst, as a participant observer, someone who at least behaves as though she belongs. My students, a handful of writers-in-training who are thrilled that it is legal to smoke pretty much anywhere in this old city, every morning talk about their evening's pursuit of the "real Prague." They've gone to the expat bookstore and the expensive disco at one end of the Charles Bridge, and a few of them are regulars at the Pizza Capri in the lobby of a large hotel near the T-Mobile Arena, or at the local bar around the corner that has a drinks menu that is like an encyclopedia of American cocktails with names like "Sex on the beach" and "Slow, comfortable screw." I want to tell them that even if they changed their tack and instead took libation at the dark and divey place near the tram stop where Czech laborers — men of girth and tight undershirts and black socks with shorts — drink beer before, during, and after work, they still wouldn't find the "real Prague." Because, after all, doesn't the presence of "the other" automatically change the game? One drop of oil in a gallon of water and it is no longer just a gallon of water.

Still, that doesn't keep my students from searching, exploring, examining the lives of others and themselves among those lives. And even though I am working, this is also a vacation for me here in another part of the world, so I too am eager to find something other than tourist Prague or expat Prague. I avoid the bookstore and the disco and even the Pizza Capri. I do, however, visit the bar that serves American cocktails and enjoy a Harvey Wallbanger in a back room clouded with smoke and a clientele of youngish, authentic Czech men and women who look at my American-loud students with some interest, and at me with curiosity. Who am I, their mother? I return their gazes and they look away, turn back to their drinks and their Czech-speaking friends.

And while I am with my students and am part of their group, here, away from my home in Chicago, away from Philip, my husband, and my cats and my smoke-free local pub, I feel painfully lonely. As the evening wears on, everyone drinks more and gets louder and I hear less in the din and pretty soon I know it is time for me to leave. The students will stay out and will later see friends they've met from nearby Charles University, from England, from the U.S., and I will be back in my third-floor room in the pension with its too-thin mattress pad on its too-hard platform bed, where I will run through the dozen or so channels on the fuzzy television set, wanting to hear English at least, but preferably American: something, finally, that I can understand. But no luck. Occasionally there is something on German MTV that was recorded in English and is subtitled in German—I saw Spike Lee's movie about the Son of Sam this way, and a few episodes of *Pimp My Ride*. Tonight, though, it is all German and Czech, and a few stations of Arabic for some reason, even though the hosts at the pension are Russian.

Each morning before class I choose a word or phrase from my Czech–English dictionary and write it 100 times in my journal. I do a version of this whenever I am in a place where the language is not my own. It's not so hard in Spain, or even Germany. Those languages make sense to me; they have roots and sounds that are familiar. Czech, however, feels almost impenetrable. So I practice my word-of-the-day aloud as I write it over and over, repeat it again and again in the tiny shower where I bang my elbows when I reach up to wash my hair. I plan my afternoon around activities where I might be called on to use these words, and I usually, as on this day, end up at Albert, doing what real Czech people do: shopping for groceries.

At the market I've found my *voda* and *meruňky*, my cheese and my bread. My arms are full and the line is absurdly long and slow moving. I stand between a freezer full of fat-marbled meats and fishes with the heads and tails still on, and a rack of Czech magazines. On the covers are photos of one of the Spice Girls and her soccer (*fotbal*)-playing husband, and of bare-bellied Britney Spears. And for some reason I'm reminded of an old *Simpsons* episode. The family walks into a megastore (here they call them "hypermarkets") and the sign above the door reads "Where shopping is a baffling ordeal." And in this line of silent and stone-faced Czechs patiently waiting their turn—as they no doubt learned to do over centuries of Hapsburgs and Nazis and Communism, and now a frenzied sort of commercialism—I snort. Behind me, an old man with bright blue eyes and impossibly white hair leans forward on his cane and smiles. I nod and grin, and body by body, we move forward in line.

Although I've planned this stop on my evening walk, I've forgotten to bring a bag. Near the cashier's counter is a wire basket of big, blue Albert bags made from some eternally enduring plastic. On it is the Albert logo and the words *váš pohodlný nákup*: your comfortable shopping. I figure what the hell—a souvenir—and decide to shell out the thirty koruna (about a buck-fifteen.) When I lift the bag out of the basket, the white-haired man says something. He fingers the fabric of one of the bags, and pulls a flimsy, well-worn clear plastic bag from his own pocket, the kind you might put potatoes in at the produce counter. He shakes it in his fist and says something else, still smiling at me. He is clean-shaven and he smells of soap; his blue shirt is neatly pressed and buttoned under the chin. His pants have a sharp crease. I smile back at him and consider the various phrases that I've learned to let people know I don't speak Czech. Like: *nemluvím česky*, I don't speak Czech; or, Do you speak English? *Mluvíte anglicky*? Or, *nerozumím*, I don't understand—which for some reason usually comes out "zeronewmean." Zero. *Nula*. Nothing. After nearly a month of living in this city, hard as I try, I still understand almost nothing.

But then the man is talking again, launching into a story about a time when he had a bag loaded with heavy groceries and the bottom broke, provisions everywhere. He tells this story in Czech, so I have no way of knowing for certain if this is at all what he is saying. But his hand-gestures and grinning and nodding and laughing make me believe that he says this exactly.

I don't stop him from telling the story. I let him go on, smile when he smiles, nod when he pauses, laugh with him. And then it's my turn to pay. I look for the numbers on the digital screen, count out the bills whose numbers are easy to read, and then the coins that I'm starting to be able to tell apart. The man behind me steps up and puts his items—a single serving of cottage cheese, three pieces of bread wrapped in cellophane, an apple, one bottle of beer—in front of the cashier. I load up my new blue Albert bag at the other end of the counter and think maybe I should say something to the man. *Dobrý den*, maybe, or *nashledanou*, good-bye. But he's already talking to the cashier, telling her the same story he told me, gestures and smiles in the exact same places. And the look she gives him is familiar to me. It's the one I've just given him, a tilt of the head, a raising of eyebrows, a nod of encouragement. It's the look I give my 92-year-old uncle when he tells me for the third time in an evening that he designed helicopters during the Second World War. The same one I give my friend's toddler daughter when she tells me a story in her secret kiddie language. The one I gave the guide on my tour of the Prague Castle, the young man who spoke not enough English for me to truly understand, but who was polite to me and eager to speak in a language he was learning. It is the same look I gave my mother during the last few days of her life when what she said no longer made any real sense. It's that look we give to any person who has something to say, whatever it is and wherever we are—the look that says we have pulled out of our own selves for just a little while to listen, to nod, to connect.

I turn away from the man and sling the Albert bag over my arm. The days are remarkably long in summertime Prague, and though it is evening, the sun still streams through the wide windows of the supermarket. I imagine my students in their rooms finishing up their homework for the day, changing into their night-out clothes. I wonder where they'll go this evening, and I wonder, too, if maybe I should go with them.

And then I step into the mass and flow of rush-hour shoppers. We move forward in a bunch, shoulders and hips bumping (touching) one another. And the doors, automatically, open for us all.

TAKING THE LONG WAY

Not that the story need be long, but it will take a long while to make it short.

—HENRY DAVID THOREAU

Our guides knew where we were headed, and we were at their mercy. The route, joined together by car parks and commercial driveways, was anything but interesting. Ten of us were seat-belted into the back benches of a minivan, our notepads on our knees, our camera bags unzipped and at the ready. We sped behind cars settled between painted lines, and passed under the low ceilings of covered lots. We were travel writers on a mission. And yet, there was nothing here to write about, nothing at all to see. Efficient, I suppose I have to admit that; the course our guides had chosen was—if absolutely, positively nothing else—efficient.

We were going to a museum of something or other (it doesn't matter now, really) after a lunch that ran later than it should have. Just outside of Washington, D.C., the early afternoon traffic was bad. More than bad; it crawled slowly like a wounded thing, stopping more than going. And our guides, eager to make sure we got every little event on our itinerary accomplished on time (more or less) had devised this little shortcut that ran alongside the major roads.

When we arrived at the Museum of Something or Other, I was eager to be out of the minivan. The lunch — an over-serving of American-style, extra-large portions and too much wine for midday — sloshed around inside me as though we were still rolling in and out of driveways, avoiding reversing cars and slow-moving pedestrians behind shopping carts. Our guides were pleased that we had arrived on time for our tour. We had reached our destination, the place they knew was the stopping point. The problem is, the Museum of Something or Other was nothing much to see, really; its exhibits were predictable and more than a little boring.

I wrote a short story once for which I knew the ending. I was young, and the story was immature, the one that perhaps many of us wrote when we were kids. Some sort of deathbed epiphany, something about too much work, not enough family, too much money, not enough laughter. If not that exactly, something pretty close to that. I was eager, like my guides in D.C., to reach that final destination. And so I hurried towards it, writing summaries instead of scenes, wanting nothing more than to get my readers to this ending with me, not worrying about what we passed along the way, or the state my readers would arrive in, as long as we got to what I now recognize as the predictable and boring Ending of the Story of Something or Other.

Does this seem like a piece about endings? About being careful not to write boring and predictable conclusions to your short stories? It is, partly, but more so, I mean for you (and for me) to consider as we write not the destination so much, but the discoveries along the way — the slow-moving traffic and wrong turns and new neighborhoods we might pass through, those unexpected places where the real story — the better story — almost certainly lurks.

I will tell you another anecdote, because this is how I make my own discoveries, by telling bits and pieces of things that may or may not be related, but might present patterns to me that I can mine for stories. I wrote a novel draft. Hundreds of pages. It was my first full draft of what I thought was supposed to be a book. It was about many things, as novels should be, as stories should be. Family. Mental illness. Loss of innocence. After polishing it up and working it over a few times, I began the humbling process of sending it around. Agents, editors. And after a while, the rejections started coming in. Good rejections, many of them (see how desperate we writers become? We develop a hierarchy of rejections from good (personal note with nice things said) to bad (personal note with snotty things said) to form letters (Dear Writer)). The good parts of the letters sent back to me said I was a fine writer, the rejection parts said there was not enough story for an entire novel. I thought they were wrong, of course. I took the manuscript to conferences and workshops; I read from it at open mics. And it was at an open mic that I made an important discovery. The book overall did not have enough story in it; the rejections were — I am sad to say — accurate. However, there was a very brief passage, two, three pages, I used over and over to read at the open mics. Here, in two or three pages, was a story's heart. And once I understood that, I took those few pages and shaped them some more and they became the first short-short story I ever wrote, and the first one I published. And I absolutely believe that the only way this short-short got written by me is because I had written hundreds of pages around it. Had I set out to write this story on its own ("The Joke," one of the stories in my first published book) I don't think I would have found my way. I needed to know more about the character—a young girl out on the streets alone at night, pretending to be tougher than she actually is—and her motivations. By living with her for these hundreds of pages, I could fully understand these complex few minutes in her life. Like Ernest Hemingway said about writing and icebergs: "If a writer knows enough about what he is writing about, he may omit things that he knows. The diginity of movement of an iceberg is due to only one ninth of it being above water."

Some might say that I am a slow study, and perhaps I am. I know many fine writers who start a story with its ending secured and are incredibly efficient at finding their way to that final destination. I also have heard more than one writer talk about the stories they thought they had endings for and with those final bits in mind either wrote failed stories, or completely changed the endings from their original ideas once they wrote more deeply into the pieces. There are any number of ways we make our stories. Alice Munro says, "In my own work, I tend to cover a lot of time and to jump back and forward in time, and sometimes the way I do this is not very straight-forward." Fine, I say.

Let me suggest this: instead of speeding through the car parks to avoid the slow crawl of traffic in order to get to the Museum of Something or Other, pull in behind that old lady in the sedan whose indicator light never gets turned off and follow her for a while, wherever she goes. See what happens when you turn when she does, where you end up when she makes her way out of the city and into the countryside where nothing is familiar anymore. And when she turns into the drive that leads to her house, follow her still, and see if she doesn't invite you in for a lemonade and a story. Or keep going when she turns, take the long road past the trailer parks and into the woods, see what creeps in the low grasses next to the highway. Don't worry about the dead ends; there is always a way out. Turn here and here and here. Keep going, keep going. Stuart Dybek, an award-winning Chicago writer, often speaks of these turnings, these digressions. In an interview with James Plath for *Cream City Review*, Dybek says this is when "the story gets smarter than the writer, exceeds his initial conception, or starts making moves that the writer doesn't think of fast enough on his own." These digressions take us away from "a nice, tidy narrative line," he warns us, but the payoff can be considerable. "There's an undercurrent to it, some kind of chemistry and interplay between the original narrative line and the digressions, that makes for greater resonance and allows the story to throw a longer shadow."

That's what I'm talking about. Consider this. You are at work on a story about a man and a woman who have had one of those arguments that are hard to survive. The type where he says something then she does, and each response gets meaner and meaner. Loveless. "You never…" "I hate the way…" "I hate you." He storms out of the house and stays gone a good long while. It gets dark; he gets drunk. The woman, in the meanwhile, has taken to her bed and cried for a bit, but then gets up to make herself some dinner. She sits at the kitchen table and sees his headlights cross the windows and hears his car's engine turn off. She hears him at the door, fumbling with his keys, dropping them, fumbling with them again. She could help him, but she does not. You, the writer, want her to. You feel for these characters now, you care for their well-being. You want a happy ending. You keep trying to write that sentence, the one in which you have her open the door for him, but you keep on writing something else. The moment, what could have been over in an instant, stretches on. He outside, she inside. She will not stand up. She will not go to the door. She brushes crumbs from the table into her hand and drops them on her plate; she straightens the napkin holder and the salt and pepper shakers. She hears him; how can she not? But she does not look up. And the man, whose point of view we get for a moment as he peers in at the woman at the table and she looks so pretty in the pale glow of the ceiling light, wonders why she doesn't get up, doesn't help him. Finally, the key slides in the lock. He stands on the porch for a minute more, about to turn the key. But he doesn't. Instead, he turns around. He walks away. Past the car (its engine still ticking in the dark) and down the driveway and out into the street. She can hear his footsteps moving away from the house until she can't. And when she can't hear them anymore, she gets up and rinses her dishes and leaves them in the sink. Then she turns off the light.

This is a detour you had not planned for the story. And there are others you might take as well. What if you went this way? What happens when you turn here? Yes, there is danger in this work, this following each side path, each unexpected turn, and yes, this process is far from efficient. You might find yourself hopelessly lost, or you might find yourself in another story's neighborhood. What you thought you were writing about might disappear like the ribbon of highway in your rearview mirror. But that is not always a bad thing, is it? I cannot tell you the number of times that I have found old, early drafts of stories that are hardly recognizable anymore. What the story started out as and what it became were entirely different things, and eight times out of ten, the thing it has become really is the better thing.

From the backseat of the minivan on that guided tour through the car parks outside of Washington, D.C., we could see other roads that turned away from the gridlock of traffic on the main streets. They ran toward green spaces and residential areas not on our itinerary to places we did not yet know. What was past that curve in the road? What did that arrow on the sign point to? Perhaps a carnival in a field that smells of popcorn and cotton candy, or a neighborhood pub where old men tell stories of days gone by, or a tree house built from purple boards and bicycle tires. Who knows for certain what was out there? Maybe nothing at all. But maybe something surprising, something unplanned. Something — almost certainly — better than what we were headed for.

"Turn here," I should have demanded. Why not? "Let's just see what's out there," I should have said. Let's see — come on — how else the story might go.

RETURNS

She sat behind the steering wheel of her car, hands at ten and two even though she was parked now, engine off, at the gas pumps. Cold dark. Winter morning. Iowa, 1980. This was home now, but not really. Home, Chicago, was a long way away.

It was my job to run the place, the small self-serve gas-station-convenience-store. A Pop Shoppe. Where you could buy soft drinks by the case only, big plastic crates, bottles to mix and match. Sarsaparilla. Lemon Lime. Pineapple. Cola. We made our money off the deposits, bottles, cases, the things never returned. The crates were like a fortress inside the shop, stacked high and wide. Syrup from broken bottles somewhere in the middle of things stained the tile floor, stuck to my shoes. There were mice. I could hear them skittering, scratching.

From my post behind the register, I saw the woman in her car. The wide front window had the best view of the pumps so I could watch when folks pulled in and out, watch for folks who took off without paying. In the mornings, I watched the light outside change, dark to light. I thought the woman might be crying; she pulled her hands from the wheel and wiped her face, over and over.

"Can I help you," I asked, leaning on the window.

Sometimes this happened: old ladies not yet used to self-service waiting at the gas pumps for someone to fill 'er up. Check the oil. Clean the windshield. The morning smelled like oats from the cereal factory nearby. Smelled like gasoline and cold.

"No, I'm fine," she (not an old lady) said when she rolled open her window a sliver. Her breath, and mine, gray puffs. "I just needed to stop for a bit." She smiled, but her eyes were shiny, red. "Is that okay," she said.

I nodded and stood up, shoved my hands into the pockets of my work coat, orange nylon and pillows of down, warm in the cold. She had a box in the backseat; it was filled with ties. Men's ties in dark and bright colors, tangled like snakes in a heap. And on the floor, three pairs of men's shoes.

A month or so after I broke up with the first man I had planned to marry, after I had decided that I didn't want to be a wife in Iowa, I wanted to be a woman in Chicago, (I was heading back there as soon as I could,) that man came to the house I shared with my brother and a teenaged girl. She was alone and (like I said) a teenager and he was a man and charming and persuasive. She let him in our house. She let him in my room.

He stole my shoes. Not all of them, not my snow boots and sneakers and flipflops, but my fancy shoes. My strappy heels, my stilettos. My going-out shoes. My dancing shoes.

He drove the country roads between the Iowa towns and tossed one shoe from each pair out of his car window. Miles of roads, a dozen shoes. And then he felt something other than he thought he would (he told me later), something other than better. So he turned back and stopped a dozen times, walked in the ditches until he found what he'd thrown out.

He brought them back to me at the Shoppe. I was working a double shift, stacking pop cases, watching the pumps. He told me what he'd done, and what he'd undone. He borrowed a soda crate and filled it with shoes. Grass and mud and gravel stuck to heels, to toes. The woman at the gas pumps on a cold, dark winter morning saw me looking.

"Want to buy a tie?" she asked. "A buck maybe?" She said, "My husband's." And, "He'll never miss them."

I imagined her husband later that morning opening his closet and finding no ties. Like I had imagined myself that night some time before, home from my double shift, getting ready to go out, looking for my dancing shoes.

"No thanks," I said.

"Okay," she said, and started her car, rolled up her window.

Back in the Pop Shoppe I could hear the mice among the bottles, hungry, searching. I watched the red shine of the woman's taillights as she pulled toward the street. She turned on one blinker, right, and then the other, left.

The morning, at its edges, began to glow.

DENTIST DAY

There was already a line when we pulled up the foothill to the clinic. Hot, muddy. The sun was high even though Honduras was in its rainy season, and steam lifted from the earth. Still, there were dozens of locals there in the brightness, snaking single-file down and away from the steps of the small, square, concrete building. Word was out. Dentist Day. The day a volunteer dentist from the U.S. would spend hours in the rural clinic shared among neighboring towns, pulling teeth and handing out toothbrushes and dental hygiene advice.

I was seventeen and far from home for the summer, an Amigos de las Americas volunteer installed in the Honduran small town of San Miguel. I lived with a partner volunteer in one tiny room of the brand new town hall, our army cots covered in sweaty sheets; the things we'd brought from home (cotton skirts, books, journals, photos of family and boyfriends, cans of tuna fish and jars of peanut butter, extra large bottles of shampoo and bars of soap) scattered over the tile floor and stacked on the two folding chairs. Most weekdays we spent going from school to school around the region, delivering toothbrushes and instructions on how to use them, pouring fluoridated water into paper cups, showing the children how to dunk their brushes, polish their teeth, swish and spit.

Some days we gave out vaccinations, pushing needles into the arms of weepy children, smiling at the boys and girls with muddy feet and unwashed hair, rewarding them for their bravery with a piece of hard, sugary candy.

But this day was Dentist Day, and the dentist, a wiry man from New York who talked fast and worked fast, was in charge of things. He didn't speak much Spanish; I spoke enough to be understood (usually,) so I was recruited to be his assistant and translator. Amy, my Amigos partner, was out front with Humberto—a local boy who had a crush on her—taking names and doing a type of triage, sorting through the people and their tooth ailments, moving the most serious cases up to the front of the line.

Did I say it was hot? I've lived in Chicago most of my life; I know what sweltering, humid summers feel like. But I was unprepared for the oppression of a Honduran rainy season, unprepared for a sunshine so heavy it pushed against my head, pressed my shoulders down. But we'd been there for weeks by this time, June 1976, (our U.S. neighbors making ready for the bicentennial celebration that in San Miguel, Honduras, we would watch in the company of some thirty locals on the one color television in town in the parlor of the doctor's home), and I had grown somewhat used to the wet heat and thick, still air.

Dentist David ("Dah-veed," he asked us to call him) was helping an old woman into a chair. With just half-a-dozen people standing, sitting, waiting, the room was tightly packed. We'd been at it for more than two hours by this time, settling people in one of three chairs, me holding heads leaned back into my hands while Dentist

David made a preliminary check of things, determined what tooth (or teeth, in most cases) needed extracting, shot the patient with Novocain, moved to the next person while that took effect, repeated the process another time, then circled back to the first person to do the pulling. It was usually quick work, the worst part for the patients the shot.

This old lady though, slowed things down a bit. She was small and brown, her black hair streaked with white, and her face softly lined everywhere except where her jaw bulged and smoothed the skin out. I understand now that she might not have been any older than I am today — in her fifties probably — but to my seventeen-year-old self, she looked ancient. I instructed her to *abra la boca, por favor*, open her mouth, please, and she did as she was told. I put my hand gently on her forehead to tip her head back and Dentist David and I looked into the cavity before us. The inside of her mouth was almost black but for an area around a clearly broken and rotted molar. There, her gums were red and shiny. She smelled of powder and soap, and the clinic reeked of antiseptic and sweat, but even through that complicated stew of odors, the stench of the woman's breath was gross, fetid, swampy. Dentist David stepped back and poured himself a cup of cool water from a thermos. He poured me one and he poured the woman one as well. We all drank, she tentatively, practiced in avoiding more pain with caution.

"*Me duele,*" the woman said and she cupped her inflamed cheek with her hand. Her fingers were very long, like an artist's fingers, or a musician's, and her fingernails were polished in a snowy pink. "It hurts," I translated for Dentist David, and he nodded and put his hand gently on the crown of the woman's head. "No shit," he said quietly to me. And to the woman, "*Sí*," he said, "*yo se.*" I know.

We got to work then, shooting her with the local, moving away to an easier case, pulled a tooth here, a tooth there, then came back to the woman. We were just about to start when Amy came into the room with another woman who carried a small boy in her arms. The boy, her son certainly, was doe-eyed and crying, scared by all of the unfamiliar pale-skinned people and the needles and tools on the tables, by the stories we knew folks were telling outside the building, stories of pain and of punishment, of toothaches and bleeding gums. The mother held one of her hands over the little boy's mouth.

"She wouldn't take no for an answer," Amy said, clearly irritated. Amy was not cut out for this work. She was sixteen, just a year younger than I was, yet she seemed childish in many ways. She was lazy and homesick, impatient and easily made angry. She spoke hardly any Spanish, having only taken basic conversation lessons during training, and when we were swarmed by the children of the village, as we were most days when we came home from tooth-brushing, from vaccinating, she pushed through the crowd roughly, and slammed and locked the front door of the city hall behind herself while I stood outside and answered their questions ("*Diez y siete.*" Seventeen. "*De Chicago.*" "*No, no tengo niños.*" No, I don't have children) and let them run their hands over my recently shaved shins, ("*Que suave.*" How soft.) play with my permed hair.

"*Está bien,*" I said to the mother and child in the clinic on Dentist Day. "*¿Qué necesitan?*"

The woman uncovered her son's mouth. He was a beautiful boy with silky, expressive eyebrows and golden skin. His hair was cut in a perfect bowl. He had a small, round nose that turned up at its tip, and just below that, he had a severely cleft palette. His top lip and gum and teeth formed an arrow upward, and his sweet, pink tongue poked out from the space left open.

"Can you help?" the mother said in clear English, a line she'd either practiced before she'd come to us, or was used to saying to whatever English-speaking visitor or interloper she came face to face with.

There was nothing we could do; I knew that, Dentist David knew that. Probably the mother knew that as well, but she had to try, didn't she? The older woman with the rotten mouth watched the small drama unfold and stood up from her chair, motioned the mother and son to take her seat. Everyone looked at Dentist David and he swiped his forearm over his brow, pulled a bandana from his jeans pocket, rubbed his neck and tipped his head to the woman and child. They sat down. Dentist David hovered over them for a bit while the mother helped keep her son's mouth open as Dentist David shined a flashlight at the teeth, the tongue, toward the back of the boy's throat. He pushed a bit on one tooth and then another, followed the line of the arrow with his fingertip. He patted the little boy on his cheek, and rested a hand on the mother's shoulder. He crooked a finger at me and I stepped closer to the group.

"I can't do anything," he said to me, but he kept his eyes on the mother and child, smiled reassuringly at them while he spoke. "I don't even know what I should tell you to say."

"And I don't think I would know the right words to say it anyhow," I said, also smiling at the pair.

"Tell her his teeth are strong and healthy. That he looks to be in good health. That he is a handsome boy. That from my professional perspective, he is fine. But tell her, too, that I am not an expert in these matters."

Dentist David started and stopped, adding another sentence as soon as I translated the last one.

"Tell her I wish I could do more. Tell her I wish them both well. I am happy to have met them."

I told them.

"Fuck," he said. "I guess that's it."

I nodded and smiled again at mother and child, and offered her a hand to help her out of the chair. She stood up, her eyes shining, and nodded at us each before she followed Amy out of the room and down the front steps of the clinic.

"All right, then," Dentist David said and turned back to the old woman who had been standing close by, quietly observing, gently stroking her inflamed cheek. "*Proximo*," he said. "Next."

The old woman sat down again and rested her head back in my hands. She opened her mouth and Dentist David went about his work, determining that the anesthetic had done its job, gathering his tools on the nearby table. He put the first of these tools in the woman's mouth and pulled.

Nothing.

The woman was so slight Dentist David nearly lifted her from her seat. He motioned for me to hold her down by the shoulders and he pulled again.

Still nothing. The tooth would not budge.

There was a flurry of activity then, a wrestling with a tool I remember as something like a small jack, a gadget meant to get under the tooth in some way, to help lift it from the gum. He pulled and dug and manipulated, and the poor woman's mouth filled with blood even as the tooth, the obviously diseased and broken tooth, held fast in the gum. We stopped for her to spit and rinse, rinse and spit. The woman said nothing through all of this, but her knuckles were the color of bone under her brown skin as she gripped the arms of the chair, and tears streamed from the corners of her eyes and filled her ears. She kept her gaze fixed on my face.

If this were a comedy sketch, Dentist David would climb onto the woman's lap in order to get a better purchase. In real life, it was as though he did everything just short of that. He paced around her head, trying to find the best angle from which to pull. He held his breath and grunted with exertion. He tugged and tugged. The other people in the chairs nearby leaned toward us as we worked, fascinated and frightened by the tooth's stubborn resistance and the dentist's unwavering effort.

And then the tooth shattered. Tiny bits of browned enamel splintered into the blood and saliva collecting in the woman's mouth. She gagged a bit and I let her head loose so she could spit the junk out.

"Fuck me," Dentist David said. He swabbed his forehead with the back of his hand, there was blood in his fingers. We waited while the woman swirled water and spat at the bucket at her side. Pieces of tooth glinted in the murky pool of fluids. My head swam. I felt woozy. She settled back in the seat again and put her head back in my hands. I held her face as much to keep from losing my own balance as to comfort her. My back was wet with cold sweat. And before she opened her mouth again to Dentist David, the woman smiled up at me.

Somehow things went smoothly then. What was left of the tooth gave up the fight, and with a few quick yanks, Dentist David extracted the remnants. The woman's mouth filled again with blood, and after one more swish and spit, I helped Dentist David pack the cavity with gauze pieces and pulled a cold, wet washrag from a Styrofoam cooler. I put it against the woman's face and told her to keep it there for a while before she got up. And then I stumbled to a bench along the wall and plopped down hard.

In my pocket I held a letter from my mother. She had sent it just a couple of days after I'd left Chicago, but it had taken two weeks to arrive in San Miguel and one of the local kids who hung around the town hall where we stayed had brought it to me that morning. I don't know how he got it. The letter was full of everyday news, of weather in the suburbs, of my brothers and their jobs and studies, of driving trips planned with friends and family, of new summer clothes, of my cat who meowed every night until my mother let her out, of decorating projects on the townhouse she'd bought just a year before, the year after my father died. It all seemed so far away. And I knew, too, in that faraway place, that home place, that my friends would drive to Foster Beach in the city each night, meet boys and drink sweet wine and cool their feet in the great lake. And there I was, pulling teeth and sticking needles into children's arms, and eating peanut butter from a jar while I sat on an army cot in my room and missed home.

With my head back against the cool of the concrete wall and my eyes closed, I didn't notice when the old woman whose tooth we had just pulled sat next to me. It was when she put her hand on mine that I opened my eyes.

"¿*Está bien?*" she asked. Her eyes were brown and warm, still glimmering from the crying. Am I all right? Me? This woman had just spit more blood than I had seen during the entirety of our operations that morning, and she wanted to know if I was all right?

"*Sí,*" I told her. "*Estoy bien.*"

And Dentist David was across the room near the chairs with two more patients, and Amy was at the door with the next in line. The old woman kept her hand on mine and it steadied me some, helped the shakiness pass. She put her other hand on her heart then, and lifted it to my face.

"Thank you," she said in English. And when she smiled, there was still blood in the corners of her mouth, at the lines of her gums. She said it again: "Thank you. *Mucho.* Thank you very *mucho.*"

Dentist David glanced at us and cleared his throat. He tapped lightly on the face of his watch. It was time to get going, I knew. I pushed myself up from the bench and the woman let her hands fall into her lap. Her face looked smoother than it had when she'd sat in our chair. I returned her smile.

"You are welcome," I said.

And then I went back to work.

I GO ON RUNNING

...

though I have built the best house I can build for you
to stop at last and rest in, you go on running.
　　　　　— From "My Brother Running" by WESLEY McNAIR

I run along the banks of the River Avon on a path shared with walkers, bicyclists, other runners. I'm an American in Bath, in England, where I've been invited to teach creative writing for four months at a local university. Can I say I live here? How long must one stay in one place to be able to call it home? Jane Austen lived here. In fact, my flat (a simple, one-bedroom gut rehab in a Georgian-era shell of buttery stone with tall windows) is on a street around the corner from one of the places Miss Austen resided. We are neighbors from different centuries. I've heard it said that Jane Austen didn't like Bath, or at least a number of her fictional characters didn't: "Do you know I get so immoderately sick of Bath...," Isabella Thorpe says in *Northanger Abbey*.

I, however, love everything about this place, starting with my morning run by the river. The path goes alongside walls built decades ago, some built centuries ago. It skirts a crescent of terraced homes curving around a wide, green lawn. It dips under low-slung bridges and passes gently bobbing houseboats. The machines of a paper factory chug noisily nearby while workers gather at a picnic table to smoke and drink coffee from paper cups. If I run this way, I reach a housing estate of lookalike buildings, dog walkers, and kids in school uniforms waiting under a shelter for their bus. If I go that way, in the other direction, I will run in the shadows of Pulteney Bridge, first built in the 1700s. I listen for the sound of wings, the heavy *whomp whomp* that I know means the swans are close by, swooping toward the river's surface. Nearly every morning as I run, I pass this pair of elegant and awesome birds, or they pass me.

I carry with me my keys, my identification, and my stories.

When I am home in Chicago, I run through the city streets that are lined with *pho* cafés, restaurants that serve noodles morning, noon, and night. There is a large population of Asian immigrants here, and the bright sound of chatter surrounds me, whole conversations I do not understand called across the sidewalks, from the doorway of the train station and the bakery, spilling out from the Asian grocery store. I am heading for the lakefront where the running path goes for miles past high- rises and restored prairie lands and beaches. I know this place; I've lived here for close to all of my life. When I first started kissing boys in cars, this was one of the parking lots where I did it, here at the foot of this beach where my run on the lakefront starts. The stories I am writing take my attention as I run, I move my lips around the dialogue I hear a character say, I try out opening sentences in my head. Unlike Bath where I run full of the wonder that comes with a brand new place, my Chicago run is like something on autopilot. I must remind myself to look up from my story-making and out over the vast and shimmering water toward Wisconsin, toward Michigan.

In Interlochen, Michigan, I run through woods and by wetlands, along the curve of Green Lake (Wahbekenetta, it was once called, "Water Lingers Again"). The dirt road I come to passes through a cottage community of summer people mostly, folks who come to this place during warm months to float and to fish, to swim and to make meals on grills to eat on decks. I'm here to write and to teach, and it is the writing I mull over on my run, while I look out toward the still, blue lake, while I feel the warmth of the sunlight and cool of the tree shadow on my face, on my shoulders. I wind through the woods and the marshes and watch for deer, for their horizontal movement amidst this vertical landscape. I can feel their presence even when I can't see them, these deer. They are like an idea in the making: There. Close. There.

Some say that writers need to be away from the place they want to write about in order to make sense of that place. Sherwood Andersen wrote *Winesburg, Ohio* while he lived in Chicago. James Joyce wrote *Dubliners* while he resided in a number of European cities, none of them Dublin. While living in Paris, Ernest Hemingway wrote stories of northern Michigan. In Bath I wrote about the Midwest; when I was in Interlochen, I wrote about Cuba, where I'd stayed in January 2000, where I ran along the sea. It wasn't until I was away from Interlochen that I could write about that place, about the first morning of my classes there when two planes flew into buildings in New York, when another crashed in D.C., and another went down in a field in the middle of our country. Some weeks after the tragedy I flew home aboard a small plane; from the window I could see below me Interlochen and the cabin I lived in, I could trace the path I ran. We see best, perhaps, from some distance.

"The runner who's a writer is running through the land and cityscapes of her fiction, like a ghost in a real setting," wrote Joyce Carol Oates in an essay for the *New York Times*.

In Prague I am not a ghost, judging from the looks I get from the people I pass. Perhaps more like an apparition, a surprising thing that doesn't exactly make sense. Every day on my run near the pension I share with my students, far away from the tourist section of the city, a place with few strangers, I pass an old man who walks a fluffy white dog on a leash. The man stops and stares at me while I run by. I nod, smile. *Dobry den.* Good day, I say. But it isn't until I've lived in this place for three weeks and made this run every day that he finally tips his head to me, that he answers me. *Dobry den.* This happens on the same day I figure out my story, recognizing as I wait to get through a crowd of locals at a bus stop—moving in place—that I have tried too hard with the tale set in a small midwestern town; I have told too much. I finish the last leg of my run—down a long hill and along a blacktopped road that leads to the door of my home-away-from home and sit down at my desk and try again.

In Johnson, Vermont, my run takes me under/over a covered bridge and for a short while on a quiet highway. I pass a small, clapboard house close to the road where I pass another old man. He has gray hair and a garden of tiger lilies that grow orange against the home's white siding. Sometimes the man sits on a metal chair, watching the world (and me) go by. We always say good morning. And then I am running on a dirt road past an old mill, a dilapidated barn, cows. There are birds and butterflies in the weeds. A loud and arrogant jay calls at me most days. I call back. I can only see so far on this run because I've left my glasses behind on my writing desk in the house I share with other writers and artists. It isn't until I wear my glasses on a walk with a friend along this same path that I see the reindeer high on a ridge. They look down at us as we go by, and I know they have watched me before; they have seen me moving my hands over the shape of a story I have almost finished, building the structure in the air, paragraph by paragraph, section by section. When I hear the final sentence in my head one day on this run, I whoop and punch my fists toward the sky.

I am lucky to have work I can carry with me, work that takes me to new places. I am lucky to have new roads to run. It is when I am in my room at my desk (wherever that might be) that I get the words on the page, but I need this other time, too, on the running path. In each new place I'm like a cat: circling and circling and circling until I can settle down. The rhythm of the steps on the road, the sound of my breath, the things I see on the way—these help me get to the story, that creative place I want to be. I run the streets I don't yet know and those that become familiar, sniffing the air, taking the long way.

I'll get there sooner or later, that place I need to be in the story. But until then, I mustn't stop, I can't give up. I will go on running.

MY FIRST BULLY

When the name showed up in my queue of friend requests on Facebook, I actually shivered. She found me. She: my first bully. With the upcoming launch of my debut story collection, I was doing what they tell you to do—reaching out on social media, making new friends, reuniting with old ones, connecting. I'd been pimping my book, too, putting up posts about future readings, interviews, workshops, etc. Friends I hadn't seen in decades—girls from high school, mostly (but not only—you know, the occasional old boyfriend who was so cute back then, small and dark—but now—now short and round and bald) were confirming my friend invitations, and others were sending me theirs. It was fun to see the pictures on those profiles. Who looked familiar still? Who had gotten fat, beautiful, successful, married, remarried, and more or less interesting than I thought they were when we were seventeen?

Perhaps I shouldn't have been surprised when she found me, my first bully, but I was. Her name is different now, a new last name with the maiden name in the middle; the first name more girly than what she went by when we were kids. We used to call her Lou. But the tight smile on her profile picture was the one I remembered from when we first met at a playground when I was what—five? Six? The time she made me sit absolutely still on one of those old swing sets with rubbery sling seats and metal chains while she twisted the swing in such a way that it caught my fingers in the links, pinching them, making them bleed. I remember her telling me I'd better not say anything to anyone. She knew how to find me. She would really hurt me.

She became a mean teenager, getting into fights in the school parking lot, performing small acts of vandalism. She'd break into cars that were unlocked and make out with older boys in the backseats. She'd open the glove boxes and spew the contents on the floor, she'd steal the toll change, she'd leave the door open so the dome light stayed on and the battery would go dead. She was from a very screwed-up home, I know that now; I think I knew that then. A single mother. Boyfriends passing through like potential buyers at an open house. She was almost certainly abused. She would make an interesting character in one of my stories; I could love her and hate her in the pages I write. Mostly, though, in real life, I hated her. She scared me.

So when I saw her name in the requests, I was tempted to hit "ignore." But I was already engaged in social media conversation with two or three of our common friends, and I figured what the hell. Maybe she had changed. I know that I have—but that's another story. Sometime I'll tell you about my own small acts of vandalism, about my own screwed-up teenaged years after my dad died when I was fifteen. I confirmed the request, and almost immediately, she started to write slightly nasty posts on my wall. One of the failures of social media particularly, and electronic communication in general, is that tone can so often be misinterpreted. Perhaps she didn't mean for it to sound bitchy when she answered my open call for workshop participants with something like "I don't care what yur [spelled y-u-r] doing this summer. Im [no apostrophe] spending it with my family." Maybe, when she sent me two or three questions in a single post and I didn't answer all of them at once, and she quickly wrote back in all caps: "YOU DIDNT ANSER MY QUESTON!!!!" [four exclamation points and three spelling errors] she meant it to be funny or something. Do you think?

But I began to feel trapped, jittery. And when she started to send me notes about my upcoming book that she had advance-ordered, telling me that I almost certainly had got our childhood wrong and she couldn't wait to prove it (despite the fact that my book is not about my childhood at all, not even set in the suburbs where we grew up) I could practically smell her hot, tuna-fish-salad breath like I could that long ago day on the swings.

She made sure to tell me when the book had arrived — writing some sneering comment that made me very uneasy but now I can't recall. I worried and waited for her response to the stories, as though awaiting a long-anticipated review that might actually matter. But here's the thing. I never heard from her again. I don't know why. I've resisted the urge to stalk her profile page and timeline to see if she is still out there, or if maybe, (forgive me, I almost wrote "mercifully" here,) she has died or something. In my own little imagination, I picture her starting to read my book (she'd be fat now, and wrinkled and in need of hair color, and her house, small and messy, would smell like wet dog and spaghetti sauce) and she'd recognize quickly that the book is not what she had hoped: some sort of tell-all memoir that she wanted (or didn't want) to have a role in. She had not been a good student. For some reason, many of my friends were not. They were interesting people with complicated families and homes, and who liked sex and drugs and good times, and who mostly have grown up well and responsible in the suburbs. I have heard from a number of them about my book, how they read it, how they liked it, how they have recommended it to others. A part of me wants to imagine that my first bully wasn't smart enough to read my book, to understand it, to know that despite the many sad stories in it, it is ultimately about hope, about love. I imagine my first bully to be a reader of happy stories, easy stories, the stories with morals and messages — despite the possible absence of these things in her own life.

I can't stop thinking about the weird anxiety that hit me when this woman showed up again. Clearly it had to do with whatever childhood trauma I still felt on some level, but more than that, I think it has to do with the insecurity every writer must feel. Once we put our work out there, it is (we are) vulnerable to whatever attacks may come, and I think, no matter how confident we are in the work, we fear the strikes and barbs of others. Writing is not a safe business. Our words on the page often leave us unprotected and perhaps even a little naked. Is it unreasonable to worry about bullies?

I have a small scar on my ring-finger knuckle from that day on the swing set a million years ago. I can still see it. It won't go away. Not entirely.

COYOTE ON THE SIDEWALK

A writer friend was visiting from North Carolina. She is a country girl, lived—at the time—in an Airstream in the woods. She posts online pictures of her view sometimes (not too far from civilization to have access to WiFi) and it couldn't be more different from mine. Trees, dense and green, mountains, and untended ground cover. Me, I have trees out my window, too, the third floor of a six-flat in Andersonville on Chicago's North side. One tree grows so close to the building that squirrels jump from its branches to a ledge outside our window, dash across that to where they can vault to the flat roof of the duplex next door. It drives our cat Pablo insane, this run of squirrels on the other side of the glass, close enough to make eye contact. The wild he can see and too, the wild it sparks in him. Philip (my husband) and I have come to call this Squirrel Highway, and we watch the show of it from our seats in the sunroom.

We—Philip, Pablo, and I—live on a Chicago side street, a place of multifamily buildings and the occasional single-family house, small strips of grass that are not quite yards. Mostly sidewalk and street out front. Cars parked bumper to bumper, except when it snows, and then, between the cars covered in heaps of white powder, shoveled-clean spots with kitchen chairs and garbage bins and yellow police-type tape (we can buy it at the Ace Hardware down the block) stretched between broom handles sticking up in the snow. "Dibs," we Chicagoans call this practice. As in: "I was up in the early morning dark and subzero Chicago winter weather to shovel this small patch of territory out, buddy. I call dibs."

But this time when my friend visits, it is autumn, early autumn, and the trees are still leafy and the air is only slightly chilled and we have gone out for a walk to my favorite bookstore three blocks away. Women & Children First, an independent that despite the odds (Barnes & Noble, Borders, Amazon) has been in operation since 1979.

We are strolling, in no real hurry, book-talking and catching up. The city bustle is behind us back on Clark Street where it never seems to stop: buses, a taxi garage open 24 hours, bars and restaurants (fine and casual), firetrucks with lights and sirens going, a small (wonderful) bodega that sells both PBR and craft beer, fresh produce and canned vegetables, expensive organic and gluten-free stuff, toilet paper and brightly colored hard candies in plastic packaging labeled with Spanish words or Asian lettering.

On my street, a small branch of Chicago's famous grid system, there isn't much going on. Middle of the day in the middle of the week. Ahead of us, a half-block away maybe, is an animal walking off leash on the sidewalk.

Dog, I think, and maybe say. A little irritated because it is without a human, and I have once been bitten badly in this city by an off-leash, un-humanned, "friendly" dog.

"I don't think that's a dog," my friend says. The animal, large, gray, slows ahead of us, sniffs things. It looks a little ragged. We cross to the other side of the road, watching.

"Coyote," she says. Or I do.

This neighborhood used to be called Uptown, but in Chicago the borders of these places are movable, depending on realtor input. Uptown was a little scary when I was growing up, gangs, poverty, and territorial divisions that made some people angry, made some dangerous. Now though, after years of encroaching gentrification little by little, we call it Andersonville, like they call the more desirable blocks with big houses and pretty graystone two-flats a quarter mile away on the north side of Foster Avenue, long ago home to working families of Swedish descent. It is a satisfyingly diverse neighborhood these days, a little grubby and a little grand, and I've lived here close to ten years.

I pass my neighbors as I walk along my street on the way to the El in the mornings. There is the paid dog walker with dreadlocks and a red hoodie and five pooches of various sizes pulling in different directions on their leashes. "Morning," I say. "Yup," he says. There are the two Asian women who tend their gardens in front of the apartment building three doors down from mine, squatting low and pulling weeds, pushing their wide-brimmed hats back from their foreheads to answer when I say hello. And there is the Cambodian Buddhist monk walking toward me, his saffron robes flapping at his legs. "Good morning," I say, and make eye contact. The first time I did this, he looked slightly startled, although not displeased. "Mmm mmm," he said in response, not sure of his English yet, or maybe not sure of me. He looked quickly away. That was a few months ago. Now, after almost daily passings, he holds my gaze, says clearly and with a smile, "Good morning." Sometimes even before I do. There is the man who lives down the street in the two-flat where a Princess Leia (rest in peace) poster facing outward used to hang in the front, first-floor window; he wears bottle-thick glasses and sits on his front stoop with a mug of coffee in his hands and nods when I say hi, smiles like we might really (after ten years) know one another. We don't, despite how close we live to one another; I don't know any of my neighbors, but I have watched them and imagined (and occasionally written) their stories for years.

My writer friend who lives in the country is a traveler. She has driven all over the United States, lived in different parts of it for weeks at a time, writing, writing, writing. She is one of those writers who does not believe the old adage "write what you know," but instead is inclined to "write what you want to know, write what you can learn, write what you discover." It is her curiosity that informs her writing, that makes it strongest. It is as if the writer in her is not fully satisfied with only what she sees out her window every morning.

I thought, when I started this piece, that it was going to be about writing, about craft. That coyote, I thought, unexpected and slightly exotic on the city sidewalk, was going to be a metaphor for the wild possibilities in even the most pedestrian (sidewalk, get it?) of stories. The extraordinary in the ordinary. And maybe it is that. But as happens with all of my writing, I don't really know what it is about until I have written it. So let me see.

My writer friend and I stand still near the grass on our

side of the street and the coyote swivels his big head toward us. He is a handsome boy (or girl) with a sharp snout that looks almost more feline than doglike; he reminds me of our skinny Pablo: pointy face, ribs like framework showing under his coat, impressively long tail. We don't move nor does he, a game of chicken on opposite sides of the road, only despite this wild sighting, my friend and I aren't afraid. We know somehow, there is no danger here. Wild is not always dangerous. Then a battered-up car with a rubber-band engine passes between us and him, and when we look again, the animal is gone.

I have written this moment over and over again in my journal. Looked at it from all angles. A couple on a first date in a short story see the coyote at night, his wildness sends them into an alley where they press against one another against the wall of a building, breathing heavily and biting one another's shoulders. A mother, already overly protective, in another short story sees the coyote and keeps her kindergartener out of school for the day. And then for the week. And then for the month. She lies to her husband when he goes to work in the morning. Sometimes, I write it simply like this: I saw a coyote today. On the sidewalk. I saw a coyote. A coyote.

I think I want it to be a sign, this sighting. Something that tells me something else I do not yet know. I haven't yet figured out what that is, but that doesn't keep me from wanting. From wondering.

And so maybe this is not a piece just about writing, but about the yearning toward wonder. (Or are those the same things?) About how living in this crowded place in the city, where noise and bustle is just a block away, makes me wonder daily — like a writer should. Who are you, I wonder when I stand on the Argyle El stop platform on an early Saturday morning and a woman in a midnight-colored, shimmering sari and a yellow down jacket stands shivering under the heat lamps; when, at noon, two tuxedoed men holding hands (obviously in love) climb aboard the 22 bus heading toward downtown. When I hear the sounds of what might be prayer from the Cambodian Buddhist Temple down the block. What are you saying? When a coyote walks casually down my city street. Where are you going? How did you get here? What is your story?

It is winter now, and the snow has begun to fall in the city. I hear outside my window the sound of shoveling, of making a "dibs" spot. I hear those sounds I will hear over and over again after the long Chicago's winter, car wheels spinning and spinning and spinning, engines gunning. That stuck sound. People trying to get out. And when that happens, I understand that, too. Escape. Escape. Like my writer friend in the woods did so often. Like the coyote did when we had our heads turned. Escape. Escape this place where after months of cold and snow I sometimes fear my wonder will freeze over.

But just a couple of days ago it was autumn, at least that's what it felt like, chilly but not cold, the earth warm enough to still be green. Where my friend lives in North Carolina, there is a drought, there are wildfires. The view from where she lives now, I imagine, is still pretty, but there is smoke at its edges and the ground cover is brown, dead. Her view, like mine, like all good views, must keep changing. A couple of days ago, it was windy here in the city, bits of paper were strewn in the grass and the gutters, advertisements for cleaning ladies, menus for delivery, homework on loose leaf blown from the clutches of children, other scraps blown from where they had been slipped under windshield wipers, or into mail slots or in the diamonds of metal fences. Now the snow has covered the scattered debris. It is white outside, the snow making everything new again, clean: streets and sidewalks and front stoops, and all the places in between.

If I stand up from behind my writing desk and look out the window, I might see the Asian women and the man in thick glasses shoveling their sidewalks. I might see the Cambodian Buddhist monk walking briskly down the street toward the bodega, his saffron robes flying out from under his parka, his rubber boots covering his bare legs almost to his knees. There will be small, wild footprints out there, too, in the strips of yards, in the middle of the street. The dog walker has been through, probably. The squirrels.

Or maybe it was a coyote.

Maybe. I don't know.

But I wonder.

RETURN TRIP

Okay, so we're on our way to northern Michigan, me and Philip—my now husband, my then boyfriend—and it's the late summer of 2003. And we turn off the interstate and there it is, the sound. The car is definitely talking. "Hit the radio," I tell Philip, and he does. Yup, that fucking sound is still there. Like the radio turned low and badly tuned. A whispering under the wheels. Ghosts.

We're on our way to Glen Arbor, where we are going to share a residency, me and Philip, him doing his painting and printmaking, me, my writing. My writing that—since our last trip up north, and with the wedding and funeral and moving and, shit, plain old city life—seems to work just like this car: more rattle and noise than anything else.

Our last time here in northern Michigan in 2001, I was teaching-writer-in-residence at Interlochen, a small arts boarding school deep in the woods and far away from the city. Philip was with me. Or, I thought he was with me. On the way up, though, he said something like, "I may not stay here very long."

"Here?" I said. "Here, here...you know, the United States"—he's British, by the way—"*here* here? or here, Interlochen?"

"Here," he said. "Um, Interlochen. Here." We were sort of living together then. Trying it out, even though he still had a foot in London, had a show opening there, would be going back and forth.

"Oh," I said, or maybe, "sure, fine, whatever."

Asshole, I must have thought. Protecting myself, of course. But still, he came with me then in 2001, he and my fat black cat, the real love of my life, Rafiki.

So it was 2001, like I said, right? And the first day of classes was September 11, 2001. September 11. 2001. I didn't have a television in my tiny, two-room cabin, so I heard about what happened in New York, in D.C., and in that field in the middle of the country when I got to school. And after I'd heard, I walked into the girls' bathroom and found one of my students there. She was sobbing, trembling, hyperventilating. Her face was white and wet.

"I have to talk to my parents," she said. Her parents were teaching in Qatar, and the girl couldn't get through on the phone. "My father," she said and gulped for breath. I patted her back, stroked her hair. "My mother."

Later that day in my cabin that smelled like summer camp—mold, wet pine needles, bug spray—I called my own mother, home in Evanston. And on her answering machine, her voice was distant, shaky. She'd made the recording after we'd got the diagnosis. Before I could start to worry, I remembered that it was Tuesday. Chemo day. She'd be at the hospital.

So on our return trip in 2003, our car rattles its way through Manistee, a Victorian port town on the scenic route up North. I always preferred this route that runs near the lake to the other way that takes you up through the boring palm of Michigan. On damp days, the sky on this side gets misty over the trees, romantic looking. It's hot today, though, and clear. The goddamn car makes a sound. And again, I turn off the air conditioner. The noise doesn't stop but the windows fog up, so I turn it back on again.

Outside of Manistee on Route 31, the car is really rumbling.

"Turn the radio back on," Philip says, like maybe if we can't hear it, it will go away, problem solved, like maybe if you pretend it's not there, it won't be. Good plan. I get it. I hit the button. What was on? "Radar Love," maybe, driving us forward, pushing us to where we want so desperately to be, the song's percussion and the rumble adding urgency to the trip.

On September 15, 2001, there were no planes flying from Cherry Capital Airport, so Philip stood on line at the bus station with the late summer tourists and students and salesmen. He was due back in London for a gallery opening, so he'd take the crowded bus to Chicago where he'd wait to catch a flight back to the place that was still sort of home for him.

A few days after that, I drove home to visit my mother. She was battling stage IV lung cancer, and I dreaded all that was to come, but that drive alone in my car on that September day was spectacular. The road was a dark vein with the trees beside it going red, going gold, going orange, and it all stunned me. The gentle slope of land and the curve of the highway as it passed close to Lake Michigan and through those small towns was almost too much to bear. I cried most of the way.

Chemotherapy was to enhance my mother's quality of

life, the doctor said. That was the best we could hope for since the disease was inoperable and incurable. *Terminal*, they meant, though no one said it. Four months had passed since we discovered what the back pain and cracked ribs and labored breathing had been caused by, and this new mixture of drugs had had a good effect on her. Her breathing was easier, she was in better spirits, less pain, and the tumor had even gotten smaller. She had her favorite nieces come to stay with her, one after the other, while I, her only daughter, ran off to another state for five months. Still, we talked every day.

"How you doing, Mom?"

"Good," she'd say, and mean it most times, I could tell even from so far away, even from my hiding place in the woods. I imagined her in her favorite chair with a game of solitaire on her lapboard in front of her, smiling into the phone. Her smile my smile. "How are you, darlin'?"

"Good," I'd say.

"Good," she'd say.

"Good," I'd say.

"Good."

She came to visit on Parents' Weekend, her last trip anywhere. She'd been a travel writer most of her life, always happiest on the road, so she understood why I'd left. Now I wanted to show off to her, read her the dozens of pages I'd been able to write in the quiet, to walk with her over my running path through the wetlands. I wanted her to love as I did the little cabin I lived in with Philip — when he wasn't off in London or somewhere — and with my cat Rafiki. But she was sick that weekend, her head and lungs thick with cold. I drove her to Sleeping Bear Dunes to look at the great lake and see the changing leaves, and she slept in the front seat beside me, snoring softly, her wig slightly askew under her hat, missing the bright yellow trees against the blue sky, the crimson weeds standing roadside. She'd grown up in Vermont, and I wanted her to see a real autumn one more time, but she didn't wake up, and I couldn't help but think, as I drove through the woods, that this is how things look when they begin to die.

On our way to Glen Arbor in 2003, Route 31 takes us into pretty Bear Lake, where we'll stop for gas and hope that the car starts up again. I can feel it rumbling harder under the floorboards. At the gas station with a view, Philip is enamored with the shimmering lake again, drawn into the memory of this place.

On one of our other trips to Michigan, I drove him through this town and showed him my dream house, a rambling Victorian with a wide lawn directly across the highway from Bear Lake. It was for sale. Philip called it "Patty's House," and he took a picture of me on its lawn. In the photo, the house looms white and huge behind me, and I'm staring out past the camera not quite smiling, like there's something that is or isn't there.

Full of gas the car starts — *yes!* — but the noise is bigger now, like a truck. No, more like a semi. So I don't even see the house when we pass, or the lake at our side, either. My eyes are on the road, what's ahead, what I want to — no, *need* to — get to tonight, tonight, tonight. A cabin. The woods. I am willing the car to make it, please make it. And I know that this might be considered praying by some, that sort of praying that those of us do even if we don't really believe in prayer. *Please make it*, I say in my head. *Please make it. Don't die don't die don't die don't die.*

On the last day of Parents' Weekend, Rafiki got sick. He'd crouch in a corner and growl, or find a warm spot in the sun on the carpet and curl into a black heap. He wouldn't eat. When my mom left, I took him to the vet. No big deal, it seemed, a urinary tract infection. Cats get 'em all the time; they kept him for a few days. Philip came back again, and we brought Rafiki home to the cabin with a big, expensive bag of special food that he wouldn't eat. The vet suggested baby food, but that didn't interest Rafiki either.

"Don't worry," the vet said, "he'll eat when he's ready."

She was a dog person, I could tell. She didn't know shit about cats. Cats do things their own damn way. Cat don't want to eat, a cat don't eat. Shit. Cat people know this.

Philip left again, and Rafiki took a turn for the worse. He barely moved, he still wasn't eating, and he stopped drinking water. I wrapped him in a towel and took him to a different vet, no more dog vet for him, and she felt under his ribs, asked questions, checked his eyes and ears and vitals and said that he had a mass in his abdomen. They took X-rays and it looked like his liver, like maybe a tumor. Exploratory surgery, she suggested. And you know how it is: when someone you love is ill, you try anything.

It turned out to be fatty liver disease, often brought on when a fat cat stops eating. Those damn dog vets. And I found myself searching the Internet for information, just like I'd done when they named Mom's cancer. It didn't have to be fatal, most said, but it often was. The vet suggested a feeding tube, stitched into the stomach so he'd be less likely to vomit. I had to go home for Thanksgiving, the last one I would get to celebrate with my family as I knew it, and so I visited Rafiki before I left. The young woman vet had given the case to her superior, a quiet man with eyebrows so blond they disappeared. He was soft-spoken, but told you everything, good and bad. My mom's oncologist was a quiet man, too. He'd stroke his upper lip and consider long before answering our questions. And when he didn't have good news about her illness, he would tell my mom and me about his family. His son was in middle school. His daughter was very musical. And on the way home from the cancer center, Mom and I talked about him; how does he have time to have a family? He always answered our pages, even in the middle of the night when Mom was fevered and throwing up, when she was too scared to let me go home until we called him and he told her that it would be okay, it was just a side effect of the chemo. "Take an analgesic," he'd say. "You'll feel better in the morning." She usually did.

The chief vet gave me his home phone number since it was a holiday weekend, and I left Rafiki, his belly shaved and wrapped in an Ace bandage. He trembled and stared at me from his cage, his golden eyes wide. He was terrified, I was terrified, and yet, (there's a pattern here) I left. And I went home to my stronger—but still dying— mother.

I came back to Interlochen a day earlier than planned after our family Thanksgiving, my chest aching from the leaving and from what I had to return to. I would pick up Rafiki and continue the tube feeding myself, even though it didn't seem to be working at the vet's.

"Sometimes it helps to be home," the vet said.

So I brought Rafiki back to our cabin home where we'd be alone. Philip was in London again, and everyone on campus was still gone for the holiday. After I'd give Rafiki his medicine through the feeding tube, he'd hobble across my writing table to push his forehead against a small, pearly boulder Philip had found on a walk in the woods. Head pressing, they call this; I'd read about it on the Internet. Animals sometimes do it when their livers are diseased. Think how often we all do it, push our head against something, feel the steady comfort of something solid. You know, like when you were a kid and you'd turn your face into the skirt of your mother, lean your head against the flesh and muscle underneath.

Philip called regularly during all of this, but he was so far away.

"Things are happening here," he'd say about his art, his show. "This might not be the right time to move."

"Oh," I'd say, "I see." My cat was dying. My mother was dying. I held the phone tighter in my hand. Soon I would be alone.

By now you're probably wondering why the hell would I want to come back to this place. Cats die here. Like Rafiki did when I couldn't save him, when I took him back to the vet to put him to rest. Mothers and boyfriends live hundreds, thousands of miles away. But here it is 2003 again, and our car is rattling toward Honor, and we pass that crazy place with the cartoon character lawn ornaments that flank a sign that says "Jesus died for us." Behind the display is a house with a sagging front porch. The closest neighbors are at least a mile away.

A man moves out to the country and no one is around for miles—this is the way an old joke starts. He gets invited by a grizzly, dirty old neighbor guy to a party. Have you heard this? You know how it goes, I'll give you a short version: "There'll be drinking; there'll be fighting, there'll be fucking." Yadda yadda. Right? "What should I wear?" the new guy asks. "Don't matter," the neighbor says. "It'll just be the two of us."

Loneliness, my friends, is a scary thing. But here's what I know now: it can be a good thing, too, being alone in the woods in a two-room cabin with snow outside and black squirrels like ink blots on white, and you're so far away from the noise of the city where planes can crash into towers and mothers can die — will die — in your arms, but not yet, not yet. And in that cabin you are warm under an afghan on the couch crying and listening to Tom Waits on the stereo. And no one can shush you, tell you not to cry when you think how glad you are that you could do something — that *I* could do something — to stop my cat from hurting, and that he, that damn Rafiki could do his spirit guide animal thing for me, so selfless, dying for me. Making me stay and face it. Giving me a practice run.

We're nearly to Glen Arbor now, and a tourist has pulled in front of us on the highway. He slows way down at each cross street, hitting his blinker then turning it off, going — is it possible? — even more slowly down the road. Our car doesn't like it slow, the rattle turns into a rumble again, and I'm back to my city driving self, cursing the other driver. Come on come on! Just make the goddamn turn! On the downhills I take my foot off the gas and it's not so bad, but when we start the slow rounding into a lakeside curve, something squeals under the hood.

"We're almost there. Come on," I say out loud to the car. "You can stop soon." The car in front turns finally, and I step on the gas, try to rev the engine up to a speed that it likes. Just a little further. Then we all can rest.

Philip, still in London, cried when I told him about the last trip to the vet over the phone, missing Rafiki, missing me.

"I'm coming back," he said, and maybe we both knew then he meant for good. And before we left northern Michigan, we decided to marry. My mom lived long enough to be part of the wedding at a small chapel in Evanston, a city reception on a perfect May day when we took photos in the Chicago springtime sun, and three months after that, I held her while she died.

When we reach Glen Arbor, we don't know where we are going. It's dusk now, but we guess at a turn, and then there's a sign for the place, and when we turn again, the motor stops, but the car doesn't. I crank the engine over and over — we're almost there, we're almost there — and it starts, and we limp the few yards and coast into the spot in front of this other cabin in the woods and we're here, we've made it.

It's nearly September again, and the leaves high in the trees are already starting their change. In the evening shadows, we unpack the car that is quiet now, no more rattle, no more ghost voices, and we leave it and go get some beers, some French fries, some whitefish.

At a table in a restaurant in the woods close to Lake Michigan, hundreds of miles from Chicago, two years from our last visit, we toast one another, the tenacious little car, the entire noisy, nostalgic trip. We don't say it out loud, but we toast, too, all that was lost. What is it about a place that draws you to it, no matter the trouble you've seen, no matter how sad you were the last time you were there? This is such a place, the place I escaped to when my mother got sick, where I could write in the quiet. The place where we drank coffee in a cool, dark kitchen the morning the towers went down, where we stood looking out at a great lake and agreed to spend our lives together, here, *here* in the U.S., where we ran through the woods on a path that circled back to our cabin where Rafiki met us at the door, tail swishing and whiskers tickling our ankles. And we're so glad we made it; so damn glad to be here. Back in this place where we've been before. Back where some things ended, yes, but back where everything else started.

THE WATER'S EDGE

My girlfriends always drove because they had cars, cool cars: a Monte Carlo, a Cadillac, and best of all, the Trans Am. Boy bait. And that's what we were there for, after all, the boys. That, and a place that seemed about as far away as we could get from our land-locked suburban neighborhoods with low-slung ranch houses and two-car garages and flat, trimmed lawns.

Foster Beach.

The City. (You could hear how we capitalized it in the way we said it, like a title, a proper noun. The City. The City. THE CITY.)

The lake was there (*is* there), wide and wild sometimes, water rolling and crashing. Wild like we wanted to be, pulled by the moon on warm summer nights. And The City twinkled in the high-rises behind us while we stood at the water's edge.

Mostly, though, we parked. All of us. We drove to the beach as though called there, a line of cars cruising slowly, looking for a spot in the lot where we could pull in and hop out and jump onto the hoods of our rides, onto the trunks. We sat in the humid dark while our warm engines ticked and cooled beneath us.

The seventies. And we were white girls from the suburbs grown bored with the white suburban boys we knew who were either jocks or freaks, and who had curfews and homework: read *The Canterbury Tales,* "The Knight's Tale;" solve for X, for Y; write a five-page paper on the Industrial Revolution.

My girlfriends, most of them, would drop out of high school, and I would go on to college, first one, then another, until I found the right one and made it work (Columbia College Chicago, just a few miles away from Foster Beach and overlooking that same great lake and the water's edge there.)

But we didn't know any of that yet.

What we knew was this: boys with names like Mario, like Ramon — City Boys — pulled huge speakers out of the trunks of their cars, played salsa at full volume, slapped their thighs and the vinyl landau tops in Latin rhythms. Clouds skittered across the moon lifting up over the water, and sometimes we would climb into the backseats of the cars with Mario, with Ramon, because they told us we were pretty. Different. And better times we would walk with them, holding hands and carrying our shoes, our toes in the sand close to the water's edge. And Mario, Ramon, would say "Let's sit, *sientate,*" and we would, and the world (or maybe just the sand) would shift under our bodies. And we'd listen to the sometimes loud, sometimes quiet lap of water on land, to the music swinging through the night from the parking lot, to the cars behind us rushing along Lake Shore Drive, toward The City, or toward Hollywood at the Drive's end.

And sometimes, too, we'd lie back with Mario, with Ramon, and kiss under the summer stars that we couldn't really see because dark is never full dark in The City; there's always light. But we knew the stars were there like we knew other things: we were young. We were pretty

(Mario said so, Ramon did.) We were miles away from home, from the suburbs, from sidewalks and shopping centers and our parents, asleep, probably, certain we were close by, safe, doing homework and sleeping over in twin beds in air-conditioned rooms.

And we knew best of all that we would come back to this place, this City place, this Foster Beach. We would leave by the backdoors of our houses and tiptoe over the patios of our yards and meet at the stop sign, the Trans Am purring, the girls inside lipsticked and ready and eager to get there. Not just the next night, and the next, but always. We would return. Pulled (even now, forty years later) by the moon, by the boys and the music, by the cars and the parking, by the possibilities, by the memories. Pulled again and again. Pulled back to the beach, back to the water's edge.

FAMILY, FAITH, COFFEE, AND THE FBI
(AMONG OTHER THINGS)

OF FATHERS, LOVERS, BROTHERS, AND COFFEE

It takes a long time to understand the language the bean uses to talk to you.

–ALFRED PEET, Peet's Coffee

On his way out the door each morning, my father would pour himself one last cup of coffee. He drank it black and sweet, three white dots of saccharin melting in the filled-to-the-rim ceramic mug. He'd carry that to-go cup out to the car where my mom waited to drive him to the Skokie Swift, a commuter train that went to Howard Street where he could catch the El to his office in downtown Chicago. The dialogue during the car ride to the end of our block went like this:

Dad: Jesus Christ, slow down, will you?

Mom: I am going slow.

Dad: Shit. Ouch. Goddamnit!

Mom: What's the matter now?

Dad: I spilled my goddamn coffee. Aw shit.

In my junior high summers, I worked for my dad in his one-man personnel placement agency. On those mornings when I would go to his office, I'd sit in the backseat and watch the coffee drama. Dad would begin to squirm. Our street was known as Bumpy Davis, a block-long section of suburban road that wasn't surfaced flat with cement. It was covered in thick, black tar that went rubbery under the sun, and this combination of Bumpy Davis and a too-full cup of coffee made for a commute of "Jesus...shit...goddamn," and by the time we got to the Skokie Swift, Dad's pants would be splattered with coffee spots, he and Mom both would be tight-jawed, and the mug would be empty (but for a few grounds) and rolling around on the floor with the others until the weekend when cleaning out the car would be added to one of my brothers' lists of chores.

There was this moment, though, each morning, when the car stood still at the stop sign at the end of our block, and Dad would be able to take a long, clean, safe swallow. Then he'd lower the mug and look out at the patches of blue sky through the trees, at the way the sun hit the picture windows of the split levels and ranch houses, at the prim, colorful flower beds. And perhaps it was this moment that made my dad face the challenge of the too full to-go cup every single morning. Perhaps it was a bright blue shining summer moment of success—of certain satisfaction at least—that made the rest of the messy, frustrating, aw-Jesus-shit ride worthwhile. But then the moment was over and we would move on.

How sweet coffee tastes! Lovelier than a thousand kisses, sweeter far than muscatel wine! I must have coffee, and if anyone wishes to please me, let him present me with – coffee!
        –JOHANN SEBASTIAN BACH, *The Coffee Cantata*

A man I met at a writers' conference tried to seduce me with coffee. The commissary coffee was notoriously bad, the color of tea and tepid. For even the slightest buzz, you'd have to drink at least a half-dozen cups. This man, a hell of a fiction writer who may one day be famous, brought his own supply of beans, a grinder, a drip pot.

One morning he found me on the deck that overlooked the lake and handed me a cup of the good stuff. It smelled like nuts roasting and tasted like warm caramel. "There's more where that came from," he said. I turned from my search for eagles in the trees on the island across the water and saw something percolating in his eyes. "In my cabin," he said. He was old enough to be my father. "This is enough for me," I said. The next morning he was sitting with the rest of the prose writers when a fluffy-but-aging blond poet leaned up against his back. She had one of those breathy voices that always sounded like a stage whisper. She spoke close to his ear. "Thanks for the coffee," she said.

At a night club in Minneapolis a man in a dark suit and a Jerry Garcia tie asked me to dance. It was a fast song, but the man kept moving close and taking me into his arms for a spin, a dip. He was handsome, with mocha skin and eyes brown as beans. When the song was over, I thanked him and headed back to my table, my girlfriends. The man followed me. "Can I see you again?" he asked. "I'm going back to Chicago tomorrow," I said. "Later tonight, then?" "I'm married," I said. "Me too," he said. And when he smiled, his sharp teeth made him look not quite so handsome after all. "I don't think so," I said. "In the morning, then," he said, "let's meet for coffee."

In a different place in the same city, a young sandy-haired musician who was drunk (but charming) wanted me to leave my friends and go to another bar with him. "I want to dance with you," he said. We were in a joint that was set up for meeting and talking only: wall-to-wall bodies; close aisles; lean-to, elbow-high railings just wide enough to hold a glass. "I don't think so," I said. "Okay, okay then," he said, and ran the back of his hand over my cheek. "Coffee, then. Let's just go for coffee." His fingers felt warm on my skin, and I'd be lying if I said I wasn't more than a little bit tempted.

In the 1500s in Turkey, a woman unsatisfied with the coffee she was provided in her marriage had grounds for divorce.

My mother has a story of when she and my father went to dinner together for the first time. The way Mom tells it, even though Dad was married to someone else, they fell in love at first sight. After dinner they sat over cups of coffee and just looked at one another. She defines true love as this moment. She says that it was at this moment that they both absolutely knew. Nothing had to be said.

During their marriage they had occasional drunken, screaming arguments that lasted hours into the night. I'd sneak downstairs and sit hidden behind a chair in the living room and listen to them hurling challenges and insults at one another. I can't remember now the things they said, except I do remember one time my mother shrieking, "He's going to kill me, my god, he's going to kill me!" After a night of fighting, morning came much too soon. I'd find my parents at the breakfast table, nursing hangovers and steaming cups of coffee. Neither would say anything. They wouldn't even look at one another.

Coffee is the calm moment.

–National Coffee Association, 1983

"Coffee?" The receptionist holds out a silver metallic mug. "Or," she says, lifting a smaller, matte black cup, "espresso, if you'd like." It's my first time in this shop, and I feel hopelessly unhip. I've come from a day of working with teenagers, conducting a workshop outdoors in Grant Park. I'd intended to run the five miles home along the lakefront, so I'm wearing a T-shirt and spandex shorts, running shoes and anklets. When the temperature rose above ninety, I decided my time would be better spent having someone chop off the hair hanging heavy on my neck than plodding along under the sun, risking heatstroke. So that's how I ended up in this new shop where the employees are tattooed and pierced and dressed in body-hugging retro bellbottoms and standing tall on platform shoes and offering me espresso. Nothing against espresso, but I prefer plain old coffee.

When I get the $700 brake job, I wait for my car in a tiny room where Jerry Springer's guests scream and throw things at one another on the television and a Mr. Coffee makes an odd whooshing noise on a rickety table in a corner. I pour a cup of coffee, but it tastes like the place smells: oily, smoky, mechanical. No one's around, so I pour the cup back into the pot.

"Coffee?" Mrs. Coates asked. A peculiar, grown-up question. I said yes, the grown-up thing to do, and she poured the dark liquid into a paper cup marked with squiggly lines and set the cup in front of me. I was in sixth grade. I wrapped my hands around the cup like I'd seen women do who sit alone at the neighborhood diner, staring out the window, waiting. The cup was cold.

The counselor reached for one of my hands. "This is hard to say," she began. I'd been called down to her office over the intercom, pulled out of base 6 drills in Advanced Math. Mrs. Coates's eyes were moist. I looked at the oily film that swirled the surface of my coffee. Mrs. Coates cleared her throat. "Your brother Allen tried to jump out a window today." I knew the words made up a complete sentence, I recognized a subject and a predicate. Why, then, didn't it make sense?

"What?"

"He was being teased in class." My brother was a senior in high school, less than a month from graduation. "I suppose he got fed up, so he went to the window and threatened to jump." Mrs. Coates sniffled. My own nose began to run. "He's at Lutheran General now."

Five South, I thought. A mythical floor of the hospital where kids went when their parents learned they were doing drugs, when they OD'd. When they attempted suicide. There'd be whisperings in the school hallways sometimes about a classmate—a popular cool kid: *You hear about Sam? Five South, man.* And it was like a badge of honor, like the stirrings of a legend. But my brother, high-strung and bespectacled, the target of teasing and jokes, was not popular. He was not cool. Allen was, however—then, and many, many times since—suicidal.

"Your mom will be here soon to get you." Mrs. Coates handed me a tissue. "Shall I wait with you?" I shook my head.

Alone in the office, I took a swallow of the cold coffee. It tasted like rusted metal, nearly impossible to keep down. One time when I was six or seven, I'd been painting with one of those long, skinny tins of watercolors. I filled a drinking glass with water to clean my brush. The color of the water became increasingly brown, and when I stirred it up, it developed a frothy head like root beer. Allen loved root beer, and—thinking it would funny—I told him that's what this was. "Drink it," I said. He took a big swig, and, as soon as he tasted it, spit it out. He looked at me through his glasses, the effect of my betrayal in his eyes.

While I waited for my mother in the counselor's office, I remembered that look. I lifted the foul cup of oily, cold coffee. "Drink it," I said. And I did.

Sometime during the eighteenth century—twelve hundred years after Arabica beans are believed to have been discovered in Ethiopia—the French attempted to improve on coffee's flavor. They added milk and called it café au lait.

The only thing I ever saw my dad put in his coffee was saccharin. In junior high once, I counted one hundred of the tabs into a sandwich bag and sold them for twelve dollars to a classmate I particularly disliked. I told her they were White Cross. Speed. Later, during home ec, she came up to me, a goofy smile on her face. "Man," she said, "I just had the biggest rush." "Cool," I said.

After I spend the night in Maine at the house of my brother (half-brother, really, from my father's first marriage. My father had six sons, then me), he makes me breakfast. We are adults, only recently acquainted. But like siblings everywhere, drawn to one another. The table is set with fresh berries from their garden, a selection of cereals, buttered toast. Next to my juice glass, my brother has arranged a variety of vitamins for me to take. My coffee is already poured and, maybe because that's the way he and his wife drink it, topped off with cream. I usually drink it black, but still I take a deep swallow. The kitchen is lined with bookshelves, there are paintings by his artist friends on the walls, small collages his wife put together of photos and mementos. Her hand-thrown pottery is everywhere, an old wood stove sits in the center of the floor. The feeders outside the window swarm with birds. In a place such as this, the warm, creamy coffee goes down easy.

I eat my cereal with juice, and when I pour my glass of apple over the granola, my brother looks startled. "I tried that once," he says. "When I was a kid. My mother beat the shit out of me for it."

My father hadn't just left his mother. He had abandoned the family. It was years before they saw one another again, my brother an adult himself by then. Every couple of times I visit, my brother tells me that once when he and our father were together as men, he watched our father with his cup of coffee in the morning. "His hands were shaking so bad, I was surprised he could hold the cup at all." My brother says he saw his father pour something in his coffee then, vodka, he thinks it was, and the shaking got better.

My father drank bourbon. And — like I said — in his coffee, nothing but saccharin.

São Paulo, Brazil. July 1975. More than half of the country's coffee harvest was destroyed when one-and-a-half-billion trees were killed by a bizarre weather system: The Black Frost.

My father put coffee grounds on the roses in my mother's garden. We had lots of things growing around our house: the rose garden; a greenhouse of orchids my dad raised; an organic vegetable garden in the back.

Whenever I had a part in a play, my father would clip

me a perfect rose. My parents were supportive of—but unimpressed by—my acting. "You were good," my mother said once about my role as someone or other. "But that older girl? That Dawn? She was fantastic!" My dad, one of those rare times he made it to my performance, would nod in agreement.

My first speech team tournament—I was entered in the dramatic dialogue category—was scheduled for a Saturday morning in October. The Thursday before, I heard my father puttering around the house late into the night. He was working on a book about career changes for teachers, and I suppose he was up writing longhand at the kitchen table, smoking and drinking bourbon. Maybe coffee. The next morning he wasn't awake by the time I left for school; we didn't say good-bye.

I see bits and pieces as I imagine that time—a house full of well-wishers with cups of coffee in hand, my mother up late and lonely drinking coffee throughout the night, me saving the coffee grounds for the roses. But I'm not sure any of that happened.

What did happen: my father quit work early on a Friday. At a market near his office in the Loop, he stopped to pick up some things for a gathering he and my mom had planned for the evening. While there (buying cheese, my half-brother has written in a poem about this, buying coffee, maybe) he had a massive coronary and died on the spot.

He was fifty-five.

Coffee makes us severe, grave, and philosophical.
                                        –JONATHAN SWIFT, 1722

Early on a bright summer Sunday morning, I'm driving

down Clark Street, running errands for a family party. It's Allen's forty-eighth birthday. There aren't many places open early in this part of town, convenience stores mostly, some 24-hour grocers and pharmacists. A small group of people stand on the corner near Wrigley Field, men in wrinkled khakis and shirttails, and women in tight black dresses and high-heeled dancing shoes. It's clear these folks haven't yet been home from the night before. One of the women holds a paper cup in her hand. A cocktail, I'm thinking, but then I see the green logo. Starbucks.

Down the street, it's cup after cup. A woman in scrubs and a ponytail at the bus stop has one; a man in shorts and sandals pushing a complicated nylon-slung stroller loaded with identical twin girls has another; the guy in the Cubs cap and *Chicago Tribune* apron hawking day-early Sunday papers in the middle of traffic, another. When I see the man in a raggedy pair of camouflage shorts, greasy bandana tied low over his wild hair, graying T-shirt scarred by holes and stains, neon orange socks and sneakers held together with duct tape sip from his Grande, I get a funny feeling.

I remember how a couple of times a week I'd meet a friend at a nearby Lakeview coffee house—an independent one with original art and fresh-baked cookies. Decidedly not a Starbucks. We'd each get a bottomless cup and return to the counter time after time for a refill. The place had a front room with a wide storefront window and a back room with a door to the alley. It was always cold in there, and we'd wrap our scarves around our necks and jackets on our shoulders and warm our hands by closing them around the thick, ceramic mugs. We loved that place. Hours would pass while we talked about men and family, about writing and not writing. Sometimes we'd share an oversized oatmeal cookie. And then my friend moved to the suburbs. One snowy winter weekend she came back to the city to take care of her sister's dog. We decided we'd go for coffee in her sister's neighborhood, and the dog dragged us to a little place a mile or so away. Pets weren't allowed inside, so despite my fourth-grade teacher's Basic Rules of Ladylike Behavior (thou shalt not eat or drink while standing or walking in a public place), we ordered to-go cups and tried to recreate our past coffee talks while picking our way over an icy cement sidewalk with a dog straining at its leash between us and cars whizzing past, the paper cups slippery in our gloved hands.

And I miss the way it used to be.

I drive further south down Clark Street on my brother's birthday and come to a rest at a red light. An empty coffee cup from the White Hen rolls out from under the passenger seat. To-go cups now hold twenty-four ounces in reusable plastic or some sort of metal, or they're biodegradable paper (say no to Styrofoam) with corrugated cardboard huggies around their middles to keep your fingertips from being burned, or they're skinny-topped no-tippers with nonslip rubber glued to their wide bottoms, and they all have caps with slits just the right size for sipping safely. And in the city, the roads are paved smooth (more or less), and the only challenge here is in figuring out how to warm your hands on space-aged material designed to keep all the warmth trapped inside.

The light turns green but I'm not in a hurry. The sky is clear and the sun is high, and I want to stay here awhile and take in this bright blue shining summer moment. But

I'm in Chicago, my city, and there's a line of cars behind me. I step on the gas, and when I do, the empty cup rolls back to its hiding place under the seat.

I drive on.

SATURDAY SHOPPING

I watched as my mother selected things we needed (bread, milk, cigarettes) and put them in the cart. I watched her consider things we didn't need but would like (steaks, orange juice, cookies), and choose a few of those as well. She calculated, the prices slipping over her lips like a murmur. I knew that when the cashier in the red smock told us the total, Mom would nod and hand over what she'd already pulled from her wallet having figured the receipt, tax and all, within change. Mom was a numbers woman; calculations came easily to her.

At the checkout, a boy in a white shirt packed our bags and the register lady said the amount. Mom handed her the money, within a couple of dollars. The lady counted back the change, giving my mother a ten and some ones (too much!) before slamming the register closed and picking up the stick that separated our stuff from the stuff of someone behind us. And my mother, for just a second, held her palmful of dollars open, but then quickly folded the bills into her pocket and looked at me, knowing that I knew. We pushed the cart over the threshold of the automatic door and across the steaming parking lot.

"You are my mother," I thought. "You are my mother."

We unloaded the cart in silence, filling the station

wagon with sacks of things mostly on sale. I felt something like sick then. Lines of sweat tickled my back. In the front seat we opened the windows to the hot outside and Mom lit a cigarette off the coils of the dashboard's lighter, squinted into the bright day, and blew smoke. She reversed slowly, checking to make sure all was clear.

We moved with the line of cars at Golf Mill Shopping Center. Saturday errands in the suburbs. I played with the buckle of my seatbelt, lifting and dropping it to make a quiet clang.

Instead of going left at the exit like she should, Mom circled the lot. She slowed in front of the grocery store and looked past me into the wide windows but kept on driving.

"Don't you need a new skirt?" Mom said, signalling a turn into a parking spot between yellow lines. She looked into the rearview mirror. "Didn't you say something about that?"

And I had. The night before she had washed dishes while I pointed out the skirts I wanted on the back-to-school pages of the Sears catalogue: the green plaid, the red. My brothers had been out somewhere; Dad was in the living room watching the news, men talking about the Vietnam war.

Mom turned off the engine, grabbed her purse, and climbed out of the car.

"Come on, then." She leaned in the window; our eyes meeting for the first time since the checkout. I looked away first. She straightened up and pulled the ten and the singles from her pocket and pushed them into her purse and tossed her cigarette onto the ground. I unbuckled my seatbelt.

The skirts were on sale so she bought me both. She spent all of the money that the woman had given her by accident. I felt giddy with it, the new clothes and the secret my mother and I held.

"Fashion show!" Dad called when we returned home. A family tradition. I put on a skirt and twirled in front of the television while Mom put away groceries and smoked at the kitchen table alone. Dad whistled and I spun until I was dizzy.

In the middle of the night I woke up.

"More money?" Dad yelled. His voice moved underneath me through the rooms downstairs. "What about the new clothes?" The kitchen tap opened and I imagined him filling a glass with bourbon, with ice cubes, with water. "You just don't know," Mom said. The argument moved into the living room and I couldn't hear any more.

I stared at the end of the bed where I'd arranged the skirts so I could look at them until I fell asleep. I put one on and stood in front of the mirror on the landing. And in the kitchen light that came up the stairs the skirt looked wrong, billowy and cheap, and the wool itched. I felt like I had that afternoon in the parking lot, sick. Sweat beaded on my lip while I folded the skirts over hangers and pushed them to the back of my closet.

I found them there the following summer. By then, I had outgrown them.

COFFEE AT THE KITCHEN TABLE
A *Mad Men* Inspiration

Two weeks in Paris, Philip and I. Him, teaching. Me...well, nothing really. I have to be away from Chicago to do nothing like this. Keeping house. Grocery shopping. Dinner. Playing Betty to Philip's Don Draper. Our own little episode of *Mad Men*, only *Mad Men in Paris*. Up in my robe and slippers making coffee, toast, and juice (but no eggs, let's not get crazy; I don't cook.) Kiss him at the door and push it closed and then turn back to the empty flat.

I sit at the kitchen table and stare at nothing. If I were Betty, I'd be smoking. Like Betty, I am drinking coffee. When I was a kid in the sixties, the seventies, a lot of moms I knew were Bettys. Sitting, drinking coffee, smoking, staring.

At a friend's house (Alice Dyer, name changed, obviously) in a Chicago suburb on a summer afternoon and there is Mrs. Dyer at the table. Did she smoke? I can't recall. I think not. She was a gum chewer. A smacker. Her hair would be in pin curlers and she'd wear a housedress. Drop waist, shiftlike thing, plaid. Short sleeves. Straight up and down.

And at Janice Brighton's (name also changed), her mother, older than all the rest of ours—Janice adopted when the brother and sister were already in junior high — at the table, too. Quiet. I don't remember her ever talking. Not like Mrs. Dyer who had a Chicago accent like those you hear on television, the vowels all flat and full of nose. (They sounded like diphthongs, those vowels, made from *y*'s and *a*'s. "Would you like uh yapple?") But quiet, old Mrs. Brighton was sad, I think, as though she carried a melancholy that held her in that chair at the kitchen table every morning, every afternoon. Staring.

On *Mad Men*, Betty Draper, even after she divorces Don and marries the rich politician, sits at the kitchen table. Funny how her new kitchen in the mansion looks like her old kitchen in the big suburban house, looks like Pete Campbell's kitchen in his suburban house. Wood cabinets and plaid curtains and harvest-gold appliances. And even though Betty is rich now (richer than before), she is still dissatisfied. Smoking. Chewing on her lips. Only Betty Draper — rather, January Jones — is a mediocre (at best) actress, and so her dissatisfied face is the same as her angry face, is the same as her sad face, as her scared face, as her worried face. Mostly she just looks a little annoyed, her lips tight (but not too tight, her lips, as a model, a big part of her beauty) and her brow slightly furrowed (careful dear, lines.)

When I was nine we moved to a different neighborhood in Niles, our suburb. A bit richer, away from the more blue-collar folks like the Dyers, the Brightons. (The dads, Mr. Dyer, Mr. Brighton, wore uniforms to work, name patches sewn on their chests.) In the new neighborhood, the mother of my closest friend (Debbie Schaefer, name changed) was more like Betty Draper than Mrs. Brighton was, than Mrs. Dyer was. Mrs. Schaefer was tall and blond, fit. Tanned. She wore her hair straight and long, in a ponytail. They, the Schaefers, had money. A built-in pool, a long, low ranch house with a fireplace that was two-sided, in a flagstone wall between the TV room and the living room. The kids had telephones and televisions *in their own bedrooms*, at a time when kids didn't have televisions and telephones in their own bedrooms. *Debbie had her own phone line!*

Mrs. Schaefer wore slacks, shorts, sleeveless blouses. Tennis shoes. She played tennis. Golf. She sat at the kitchen table and smoked. She yelled. "Debbie, get in here!" "Johnnie, the dog has to go out!" Like it was too much trouble to get up and walk through the house to talk with her children. She swore.

Mrs. Schaefer gave us rides to school, although we lived close enough to walk, certainly to ride our bikes. I can still picture her sitting in her Cadillac on the side of our blacktopped suburban street, window rolled down, blowing smoke into the daylight, staring straight ahead, waiting for me to run out the door and jump in the backseat with Debbie. Once, I had a friend from the city staying with me while her parents were traveling, and I brought her to school. When we got in the Caddy, Mrs. Schaefer muttered: "I knew it." What she meant: Sybil was black. In our lily-white suburbs there were no black families, but Mrs. Schaefer knew that we, the McNairs — the rabble-rousing Democrats who held fundraisers for progressive candidates and had an organic garden in our backyard in the middle of the flat green lawns and neat flowerbeds stretched up and down the block; the McNairs who both had jobs (*Mr. and Mrs., for chrissakes.* And she, Mrs., wasn't just a secretary or a bank teller or a cashier, but did something with books, worked for a publisher); the McNairs who helped their oldest children, the high school boys, organize protests against the school dress codes, against the Vietnam war—these McNairs, my parents, my brothers, me...well, of course Mrs. Schaefer knew my friend visiting from the city of Chicago would be black. Wasn't everyone in the city black?

In *Mad Men*, for a long, long time the only black characters were elevator operators, domestic help. Carla is Betty's long-suffering maid while she's married to Don, she is the only adult in that house who might help the kids grow up okay. Poor Sally, Bobby, and Gene, the baby who seems to be taking forever to get any older, who most viewers (or is it just me?) could never pick out in a baby line-up. Fleshy, white, indistinct. Don is a drunk and a philanderer and has gone as far as to tell people that he doesn't know how to love his kids. (Didn't he say something like that? Who did he say that to? Megan, his pretty, young, new wife? That blond psychologist Faye he was sleeping with for a while?) And Betty, who is mostly just stupid and spiteful and mean. Without Carla, these kids would never have had a chance.

Of course, Betty fires her.

When I was a kid, since my parents both worked and we could afford it (but we weren't rich like my friend Debbie's family, no televisions and telephones in our bedrooms) we had help. We always had help. When I was really little, when we lived in our blue-collar neighborhood, we had Sandy (her real name, but that's almost all I remember of her. A white girl who was more babysitter than maid). And then Mrs. Deece (also her real name because I loved her). She was a plump black woman who (I still remember this; I always and often remember this) had the softest hands in the whole wide world. I can still feel them on the back of my neck from when she brushed my hair, pulled it into a ponytail. And she made us fried bananas. These might be the best things I have ever eaten. Not fried plantains, like a starch, but sweet, brown, ripe bananas battered and fried and served with syrup. Yum.

When we moved to the new house, we got a new cleaning lady. Mrs. Deece, I think, got a better job. When did we start calling them cleaning ladies? "Cleaning lady," a tidy little euphemism for maid. I don't think we ever called these women "the help," or like Betty and her friends do, "the girl." Our new cleaning lady was Mrs. Bristol (real name). Eileen Bristol. She was from British Honduras, Belize now. And years later when I visited Belize as an adult, I imagined Eileen Bristol there in the dusty streets and sunshine. When she worked for us she lived in the city, Chicago, in a small apartment on the North Side by herself (probably close to where I live now). I visited her there at least once. She had a son in British Honduras then. A teenager, even though she wasn't very old. The first time, when I was in junior high, I did the math of that—mother, thirty-something, son, teens—I understood that she was about the same age as my brothers were right then. High school aged when she gave birth to her son. She told me she'd come to Chicago to give her son a better life.

We picked up Mrs. Bristol (Eileen, she wanted us to call her Eileen, and now I think she may not even have been a Mrs., may not have been married) at the convenience store near my grade school on Saturday mornings. There were a number of black maids (cleaning ladies) there waiting for rides on Saturday mornings; it was the last stop on the bus from the train. We dropped her off there, too, in the afternoons, at the end of her one workday with us.

Do you remember the cultural shift in *Mad Men* when they started to hire blacks at the ad agency? It began as a joke during serious times, the civil rights era. Bags of water dropped from office windows on black demonstrators, a bogus help wanted ad in the paper. But then, when Don's reception area filled up with blacks (African-Americans) looking for work, the agency had to make a token hire. By the end of the last season, Dawn, that hire, had moved up the ranks to office manager.

The times, they are a-changin'.

My parents were actively engaged in civil rights. I've read journals of my mother's and she's told me stories about how she broke with the church when she lived in Washington, D.C., because one of her black friends was not allowed in my mother's white church in the fifties. My folks had a hand in finding and hiring the first black staff member to our suburban school district in the midsixties. Sybil's dad became our librarian, and Dr. Mack, her dad, became my parents' friend—which is how I became friends with Sybil and how she came to be with me in the backseat of Mrs. Schaefer's Cadillac, just like Mrs. Schaefer knew would happen. The only other black person, probably, ever to sit in Mrs. Schaefer's Cadillac would have been her cleaning lady. (And why did she need one, anyway? She was home all day. Why did Betty Draper need one? So she could sit at the table and smoke some more?)

As I got older, I began to consider how my folks squared having black help with their civil rights rabble-rousing. Did they think they were helping this way, by being job providers? Were Eileen and the other black women huddled at the door of the convenience store, waiting for their rides to Saturday morning work, the only domestic help available then? Were we, as perpetrators of the stereotype, white suburban families with black cleaning ladies from the city—part of the solution, or just another part of the problem?

I wonder if this is the sort of thing that Betty Draper sits at her kitchen table thinking about after she makes breakfast for Don, after she kisses him and sends him off to work. Like I just did for Philip. The sort of thing I think about now, during these two weeks when I am not working and Philip is and we are in Paris. Alain de Botton said, "It is not necessarily at home that we best encounter our true selves." So I sit here at the kitchen table—in this place that is not my home—with my coffee and I think about that, too. I think about wives at kitchen tables, about television ones and real ones. And how even though I am not Mrs. Dyer, Mrs. Brighton, Mrs. Schaefer, how I am not even close to being Betty Draper, here I am, sipping coffee, staring.

I am curious about so many things. About women in the world. About wives and mothers. About what is help and what isn't. About black and white. About what's on television. And at my kitchen table in Paris, a place from where I can see Chicago, see home more clearly perhaps, I pour another cup of coffee. I pick up my pen.

ROGER THE DODGER

Make the most of your regrets; never smother your sorrow, but tend and cherish it 'til it comes to have a separate and integral interest. To regret deeply is to live afresh.

—HENRY DAVID THOREAU

Among my mother's things, our progress reports. Midsixties, and so, in the spirit of progressive education even in the public schools of Chicago's suburbs, these records of our achievement and potential were renamed—not "report cards" (is this too Big Brotherly? Too Orwellian? Too McCarthy-esque?) but "progress reports." And here, some fifty years later, I can't help but note how little, really, progress we (my brothers, Allen, Donald, Roger, and I) have made. Donald is still "bright" and "organized." Allen demonstrates "both thoroughness and insight in his study." I am "well-behaved" and "a good reader and writer." And Roger, dead now for more than six years, was always "jolly."

Everybody loved Roger. Despite his weight (well over 500 pounds at his death), despite his propensity to borrow money and not repay, to always be in some sort of need. Like so many of us in our family, he was probably emotionally—let me say—*compromised*. I remember he went for counseling when he was an adolescent, but I don't remember why. He had begun running away. He hitchhiked to the next state and joined a carnival when he was fourteen, the cops brought him home. He was food dependent, pleasure dependent, then and always. He spent more money on gadgets and services than he could afford, more than his real expenses (a home, clothing, his taxi lease) would allow. A man who never fully evolved into grown-up responsibilities and self-care. Roger the Dodger. But man, did he know how to enjoy himself.

No one, no one found as much joy in Chicago — this city that was hard on him, hard for him — as he did. The pretty city women in their summer dresses passing the nose of his cab. He was one of those guys, the kind who would whistle at women, who would yell out his window *Looking good, Lady!* He was not a predator, he was not a threat, not dangerous, not even a little. He was vociferously moved by beauty. He was joyful. Appreciative, especially of this city and all its offerings. As a teenager he knew his way around on the subway, on the El. When he learned to drive, he explored every neighborhood. He knew all the shortcuts to get around traffic on the Kennedy, on the Tri-State, on Michigan Avenue. As an adult, he would park his cab near the lakefront and watch the blue sky and glittering waves in his windshield until he dozed. (This was when he didn't have a real home, when he spent some nights — if he could afford it — in transient hotels, when he carried everything he owned, a jumble of papers and electronics and cords and mostly clean underwear and packages of cheap cotton socks stirring around in a couple of Hefty bags in the trunk of his cab.) He would program alerts on his phone to let him know the score of Cubs games; he would cheer loudly when they won. (How he would have loved the World Series win.) He would take photo after photo every year of the enormous Christmas tree and its lights in Daley Plaza. Those pictures, like the Christmas trees themselves, all looked the same to me.

Roger drove the Santa Cab. Was this his idea? He had been a cab driver since he was a teenager in the suburbs, plus, he was always rotund. He loved Christmas, his birthday came just two days following it. So during the holidays, he would put on a Santa hat and a fake white beard, and drive his taxi around. He would *Ho, ho, ho,* anyone who got inside his cab. *Merry Christmas,* he would say, pitching his voice low like the Santas of cartoons. This is how it started. A red hat and a white beard and a standard line.

Years into his work driving cab, the company he drove for caught on. They helped him pay for a full Santa suit (he was close to 400 pounds by then) and for decorations. Colored lights strung over the ceiling and around the windows of his cab. A sound system blared holiday music out into the streets from a speaker on the taxi roof. If you were lucky enough to catch the Santa Cab, your ride was free. This wasn't his idea (he usually was broke, remember, so free wasn't something he would have proposed) but it got great publicity. He was in the local newspapers and on *The Today Show,* and during those days, he had the time of his life. Happy customers, generous gratuities, national celebrity. Ho, ho, ho!

Boy, he loved driving. Even as a little kid, Roger was a driving guy. Hours and hours on the floor of our den with Matchbook cars, making those spitting engine noises that kids do. He studied to be a truck driver, and passed his licensing tests, but he had no way of investing in that career. When I moved to Iowa for a short while in my early adulthood, Roger followed me. (We were always very close. When we were little kids, five and seven, I cut my hair short as a boy's and pretended we were twins.) In Iowa, he drove a school bus.

And he stripped.

Do you remember the male stripper craze of the seventies, the eighties? Chippendales, that sort of thing? We had our own local troupe of male dancers in Cedar Rapids, Iowa. Guys who loved to dance and were good at it. Guys with good enough bodies. They invited Roger to join them, all 300-plus pounds of him then, and gave him a pair of triple-XL boxer shorts with red hearts. They called him Buffy, short for Buffalo in the Buff. He danced (not very well, but with great enthusiasm and delight) and took off his clothes and people laughed and sometimes, and these are the good times, he got laid, just like the other male strippers did. He loved stripping. Almost as much as he loved driving.

It—the stripping, not the driving—embarrassed me.

Roger loved loving. "This Guy's in Love With You" by Herb Alpert was his favorite song. He had a handful of women friends when he moved back to Chicago and started driving a cab again. Needful women, most of them, living close to crisis (Kim, whose boyfriend beat her often enough to finally land in jail for it; Tiffany who was evicted from this apartment, then that one; women he met online and in the back of his cab who couldn't pay for their phone bills, for groceries, for the rides he had just given them), and he called them each his wife. His phone would ring (the latest of many gadgets he bought, always the newest, the best, the bells-and-whistle-iest that took whatever money he made so he couldn't pay his own rent, couldn't pay his parking tickets, was always late on his cab lease) and he would say to whomever was in his backseat, "That's my wife calling." In name only. I don't think he ever even made out with any of these needful, emergency-prone women. They certainly never conjugated their relationship. But he was an easy touch, and whether he could afford the time or the money or not, he would try to help. He wanted to be a savior. *You see this guy*, his favorite song goes. Roger—this by now 500-pound man who most people looked away from—wanted at the very least, to be seen.

Roger was fifty-three years old when he died. A summer night. Chicago hot. I woke up in the middle of that night with a pain so sharp and expanding in my gut, I was afraid I might explode. But I didn't, and I fell back to sleep, in the bedroom with the door closed because we had the window air conditioner on. I woke up a couple of hours later, a little achy, in need of the bathroom. When I opened the door, I heard an odd mechanical voice coming from the answering machine. "He may die." That is all I heard.

I have regrets.

I regret that when we were children on a plane flying with our family from Spain to Portugal, while he slept I took the postcard Roger had written to our grandparents from the seat pocket in front of him and erased what he had written. He was a lefty and dyslexic (although we didn't know that then) and the card was messy.

Misspellings and sloppy handwriting and extra letters at the ends of words X-ed over. I erased it and rewrote it. In my pretty, little-girl cursive. Even as I did it, I felt sort of squirmy. Why did I think that what he had to offer was not good enough?

Before I even replayed the message on the answering machine, I knew it was about Roger. My oldest brother Allen was texting from the hospital, and the message was played into my machine as a voicemail. It was city dark in the apartment, shadows and light coming in the windows. The light on the machine blinked yellow. Caution. Caution. Caution. There were three or four other messages. Allen had been calling regularly for a couple of hours. I began screaming. "He's dying! He's dying! He's dying!" Philip jumped out of bed, ran to me. "What? What?" (Later he would tell me that he thought I was yelling about one of our cats.) I couldn't stop shaking.

Roger was an easy crier. Like our mom, like one of our nephews. A mush, we used to say. He cried when he sang with his favorite song: *you see this guy...* He cried at *Miracle on 34th Street*, at *It's a Wonderful Life*. He cried once when he was particularly broke and working night and day driving his cab and so not getting enough sleep and hit the front bumper of a van when he tried to parallel park.

I cried when people made fun of him. When we were kids. When we were adults. I cried when his "wives" took advantage of him. When anyone did.

And they did.

One of the Hefty bags of Roger's things I picked up from the nursing home where he lived his last month was full of his few pieces of enormous clothing. I left that bag behind, told the nurses to throw it away. The other bag was full of his gadgets: a half-dozen cellphones, working and not; a laptop; hand-held electronic games; a couple books (Harry Potter series); ID cards and papers; expired cash cards and cancelled checks. Some he'd written returned for nonpayment, and one dated around the same time—just a couple of weeks before he checked himself into the nursing home—to him for 2,000 dollars, also marked "Insufficient Funds." The payer on the check, some bogus tech company. And I could imagine what happened. My brother had fallen for a scam promising to send him money for something—a survey maybe, or trial use of a phony product—and he'd written checks on outstanding debts believing that the check for a couple grand was good.

Was that why he'd checked himself in to assisted living? A means of escape, perhaps?

The weeks before he died, I was traveling. I spoke to him every couple of days by phone. The nursing home he was in was paid for by federal and state safety nets, and he was hungry but excited because they had him on a low-calorie diet. He imagined his life in just a few months when he would be skinnier, healthier, able to return to an existence more traditional than the marginal one he had survived so far.

I visited him before I left. The place was less than a mile from my apartment, in an Uptown neighborhood. It stunk of boiled vegetables and soiled bedding and pine cleaner. Roger spent most of his day in bed, watching television, fiddling on his computer, flirting with the nurses. He was not bored. He was not unhappy.

When I was in Cooperstown, New York, researching

a travel article and walking around the Baseball Hall of Fame without much interest, Roger got sick. An infection in his gut. They took him to the hospital. He spoke to me from there. He cried over the phone to me because they wouldn't tell him when he could leave. He was afraid he would lose his bed in the substandard facility where he probably got sick in the first place. When, a day later, they released him and sent him back to that place, he left a message on my voicemail, I heard it on the road. He was laughing, relieved, homebound.

I called him for two days as we drove back home. He didn't answer my calls. I left messages. I got pissed, like a sister will, because he didn't call me back. When we arrived home, I called again. After thousands of miles and days away, I had returned. We were close. I was just a mile from him. I could have walked over there. I thought I should. But I didn't.

As I said, I have regrets.

Roger died in an expensive hospital near Chicago's lakeshore. Whenever I run or walk along that stretch of lakefront path, I have to look away, stare out over the water, blink back the tears. He died of the same infection he already had, gone to sepsis, untended by the people at the nursing facility.

We were there. My brothers Allen, Don, and I. The critical care nurses who took care of Roger in his last hours were young and beautiful. They leaned over him as he struggled to breathe, in a coma, as his belly swelled even more hugely. They wiped the spittle from the corners of his mouth with cool towels; their hair pulled back in loose ponytails swung over their shoulders; their smiles were kind; their touch was gentle. They spoke to him in quiet voices. Like lovers.

You see this guy?

Oh, how he would have loved that part.

When Roger the Dodger moved back to Chicago from Iowa, he left behind significant debt; the memory of his pet dog who died because (he told me) he could not afford to feed him; friendships that had grown cold because people were weary of supporting him; garbage and gadgets in the motel room where he'd been living for the last few of his Iowa months. Back in Chicago then he was homeless, mostly. Sometimes he stayed with friends, sometimes at SROs, sometimes with our mother, sometimes with me. We would go out together sometimes, to a dance club on Division Street where I worked as a bartender, a waitress, an office manager, depending on the day. We were young, Roger and I, so we drank young, stupid drinks. Long Island Iced Teas, Tequila Sunrises. We would get drunk, and Roger would get loud, singing off-key, banging on the bar, dancing like he did when he was a stripper, and I would get embarrassed.

I cannot smother my sorrow. I regret deeply, many things: I did not walk over to the nursing facility when Roger did not answer his phone. I did not, when I could have, help him live.

But mostly this: at the bar on Division Street when we were both drunk, I told Roger to shut up, to quit making so much noise, to settle down, to keep still. He looked at me chastised, hurt. His eyes filled. "I'm just trying to have a good time," he said. "Just trying to have some fun."

And I regret deeply, with great sorrow, that I tried to stop him from that.

CLIMBING THE CROOKED TRAILS

"Climbing the crooked trails…" my grandfather, Victor Hugo Wachs, wrote about his experience on the back of a motorcycle in Korea in the beginning of the last century, the place he had been assigned to carry out mission work by The Korea Quarter-Centennial Movement of the Methodist Episcopal Church. I found this line among his letters, the ones from the boxes in my mother's apartment.

Sylvia (my mother) died in 2002 after what was both a long and much too short illness. We knew it was coming for more than a year, so we had time to plan, to talk, to get things sorted. Still, after her death, the task of going through her things (the things of a seventy-eight-year life) was overwhelming. Not just what to keep, what to share, what to discard — but the discovery of all there was. And, more specifically, all there was *left*.

Boxes of letters and photos and negatives and documents and bits and pieces that my grandmother passed on to my mother. Decades of correspondence from my mother to hers, and decades of correspondence from her parents, from my grandfather mostly, to people I knew and didn't, and to and from places I'd never been. Things written before and after the birth of my mother.

My mother was a writer; she told me that I needed to write, too. She gave me assignments, small writing prompts, when I was a little girl and while she worked at her editor's job. In summer and on school's-out days, I would write stories for her. This collection of writing is like another assignment left to me by my mother.

My mother was born in Korea. I've always loved telling people that. It's a cocktail party line, a thing I say to make myself sound like I have an interesting past, something to tell. Something more interesting than the truth: despite a short list of places I've called home, I've lived ninety-eight percent of my life in the Midwest. In fact, today I live less than a mile from Chicago's Edgewater Hospital (closed now, fallen into disrepair) where I was born.

But my mother was born in Korea. When I tell people that, there's often a hiccup in the conversation, a squinting of eyes over the highball glasses by my fellow cocktailers.

"Are you Korean?" Someone usually, invariably, disbelievingly will ask.

Look at me. I'm a mutt, like most Americans. A bit of that, a bit of this. A smidgen of French. Ancestors from England, Scotland, Germany, Ireland. My hair shines reddish in the sun. I freckle. I am not Korean.

When I was little, I thought I *was* Korean. I thought that being born someplace meant that you were of that place, you could name yourself when you named the place, and, consequently, you could name your children that, too. Your grandchildren. How many of us are called American, despite our origins, our ethnicity, our lineage?

"You're not Korean," my mother told me once when she heard me say to a playmate that I was.

"You are," I said.

"No I'm not."

"But you were born there." How old was I then? Whom did I tell? It might have been Janice Brighton, the little blond girl who was adopted and lived next door. The girl who was prettier than me, who had her own room while I still had to share mine with my brother. What did I have that she might not?

"I was born there," my mother said, nodding, ironing. She had a day job, but I remember her standing in our kitchen, ironing. "Still, I'm not Korean. And neither are you."

We are not Korean. I am not Korean.

Chicago, Illinois. Bath Spa, England. Mount Carroll, Illinois. Cedar Rapids, Iowa. Interlochen, Michigan. San Miguel, Honduras. Niles, Illinois. Mount Vernon, Iowa. Prague, Czech Republic. Johnson, Vermont. Solon, Iowa. Florence, Italy. Paris, France.

These are the places I have lived. Some for years, some for weeks, a month. Places I've called home.

8855 Greenwood Avenue. My first address. 299-3165. My first phone number. A series, each, of digits set to memory so that I could use them to find my way, if need be, to the place I grew up. The first place I'd ever really been.

I've been thinking about the idea of place—I often do—and the idea of being in a place. Of being placed. Not just my situation, where I am situated, but also that other sense of place. As in the abstract, emotional way of place. Like: "Let me tell you where I am at with this." And the logical, debatable, pro and con of place: "This is my position." "Here's where I stand." To me, these ways of considering place (physical, philosophical) are inextricably bound together. Despite my having been a travel writer (like my mother) and having over the years taught in four different countries, there are many, many places I have never been. Among these is Korea. And yet, from reading my grandfather's letters, I have visited this Korea of my mother's origin, of my grandparents' and aunts' and uncle's lives in the early 1900s. This is not a place that exists any longer, not exactly as it was then, and yet I visit it, again and again.

My grandfather, so the family lore goes, was the first person to ride a motorcycle in Korea. That's a version of our history I believed for years. Decades. Here's a modification of it: my grandfather was the first non-Asian to ride a motorcycle in Korea. That may be closer to the truth, a truth I might be able to find if I did the research. Internet. Books. Records of motorbike sales. Etc.

I have to admit, though, I'm not really interested in the truth. Not in this case. I am much more interested in the lore, the mythology of such a claim. A white man (Victor Hugo Wachs) named after a poet, on the seat of a motorcycle traveling over the hills and rutted roads of early 1900s Korea, a Bible in his rucksack, a baby on his back, and my grandmother wrapped in her skirts and settled in the sidecar.

Does it matter if he was the first rider there, the second? The twentieth? The story, to my mind, is spectacular, incredible enough without any more heightening.

My grandparents were missionaries. I was never baptized.

My father died when I was fifteen years old. He was an atheist. His parents, like my mother's parents, were Methodist. Evangelical.

My father was an atheist and I was never baptized, and my mother, who was born in Korea to missionary parents, had her own doubts and split with the church in her twenties.

So when my father died when I was fifteen, when he was fifty-five, I thought, though I didn't know, that if there was a god, a heaven and hell, my father would be going to hell. Despite his having reared and loved a family, despite his having worked on causes, social issues, despite his propensity for occasionally taking in strays — people without family or direction — to live in our home (good, Christian work, all of this), my father, the atheist, would go to hell.

I've been thinking about the word *CHOSEN*. It's all over my grandfather's letters, and I suppose I am a bit embarrassed to admit that until recently, I hadn't known that it meant KOREA.

It's an interesting word. Full of meaning and possibility. To choose. To be chosen.

Chosen. I wonder if all those times my grandfather wrote that word at the top or the bottom of a letter (addressee, signator) he even noticed the American word behind it.

Chosen. Selected.

Did he feel chosen to be in Chosen? Or did he choose this place to be?

Chosen. To have a calling. To be called. To be chosen. To be in Chosen.

Among my grandfather's letters is one from my great uncle, my grandfather's brother Paul. I remember Paul slightly. To me when I was little, Uncle Paul looked just like my grandfather, only slighter, shorter, perhaps. Or maybe taller. Thinner. I have a shimmery image of him standing near a car in a church parking lot, smiling in the sun even though it is—of this I am sure—a funeral day; whose, I don't recall. Grandmother's? The memory is not fully there, like some of the photos I've found, bright and shadowed in a way that makes me not certain what I see. I remember liking Paul immensely, finding him funny and kind and warm in a way that was genuine to my child way of knowing things.

In his letters to my grandfather in Korea, Paul speaks openly and with great concern regarding his doubts about faith, about God, about his own calling.

These letters from Paul are among my favorites among the hundreds. The uncertainty attracts me. The things he does not know. The things he may or may not believe. His place in a world he does not fully understand, may not trust, cannot be sure it is as it appears.

This is a place I know. The place between doubt and commitment, between knowledge and faith, between stay and go.

Paul became a minister despite his doubts. Or maybe because of them.

I want to say something more about when my father died.

I remember that some days after his death I was sitting in a car in the parking lot of a Kmart, waiting for my brother or my mother to return from running an errand. It was autumn, cool, and dark in the evening. My father died in October.

An Asian girl approached the car. She had pamphlets in her hand. She was a Moonie. A follower of Reverend Sun Myung Moon. A Korean missionary of a sort herself, I suppose.

My window was open, and so she stopped, looked in. Teenager to teenager. She didn't speak much English, but she said something about God, about Reverend Moon, about heaven, maybe.

I had been struggling with the idea of my father, my good father, going to hell. And so I asked her, implored her to tell me I was wrong, to explain it to me if I was right, why, how. To make me feel better about things.

The more I spoke, the less it seemed she wanted to hear. Perhaps it was because she didn't understand my language, or perhaps it was because she didn't understand my pain. She looked frightened, I remember now, scared of whatever it was I wanted.

And what did I want? Kindness, maybe. Comfort, certainly. Reassurance, yes.

The girl backed away from the car window and said, "Call this number." She pointed at a pamphlet, one like she had given me, one I didn't recall taking but found in my hand. "Call this number," she repeated. And even as she said this, it sounded to my ear like she was speaking from memory like you sometimes do when you learn a new language. Answering by rote.

I carried the pamphlet with me until I didn't anymore. I never called the number.

My mother and I, in the last years of her life, talked about assimilation. It was after that particular September 11th, and there was fear everywhere, a distrust of "the other."

She surprised me by saying that she thought people of different cultures should try to fit in to the culture they inhabit. Assimilate. My left-leaning mother with very few prejudices thought we should all try to blend in. In practice, I know this desire, to look like you belong, to not be the obvious interloper. Though I am a regular tourist, a frequent visitor to places other than my midwestern home, I am not eager to call attention to myself for this and the various ways I am different from the locals.

Sometimes I can pull this off. The many summers I taught in Prague, for instance, I walked the narrow city streets with purpose, planning my routes ahead of time as much as possible, pretending I knew where I was and where I was headed even if neither of these things was true. And I wore a Czech scowl. There is a certain dourness to Czechs — at least in Prague, but I've seen it in smaller towns, too — that middle-aged residents wear on their public faces. More than once I was asked directions, tram information, questions I couldn't understand, much less answer. And not just by tourists, but by locals as well.

I had assimilated.

But consider this: my grandfather in trousers and shirtsleeves and cap, goggles over his eyes, astride his Harley or his Indian (depending on the year) motoring into a tiny Korean village. My grandmother in flowing Victorian skirts, petticoats underneath. Her fine brown hair pulled up under a wide straw bonnet. Their four children, blond and grey-eyed and easily burned by the sun. Playing Ring Around the Roses and London Bridges Falling Down.

Could they be more "other" than their parishioners, their Korean hosts? Could they be any less assimilated?

I am surprised and a little dismayed by the lack of information about my grandfather's children in his letters. My mother was born in Korea in 1924. Her older sister Marie Evangeline was also born there. Her brother Miller, too. El Rita, the oldest child, a girl, was born in the United States and carried to Korea in 1910.

Wasn't there something to say about these little American children among the Koreans (and Japanese, soldiers mostly) in this tiny Korean town?

"The baby has been sick," in one of the letters.

Which baby, I wonder.

My mother told me about a time when she came back home to Vermont where her family had moved after her parents' sixteen years of mission work. This was years after they'd arrived back in the States, sometime after she'd left home for college, for jobs. She'd been working in Arizona in a Japanese relocation camp. Keeping records for the government, hoping, in this time of world war in 1943, that her work with the Japanese might be meaningful, helpful — in the way so many people wanted to be useful then. Her infancy connected her to Asia and Asians, but she didn't know at the time, or didn't want to believe perhaps, how wrong the Americans were in this relocation, this internment process. How vengeful were their motives. How racist.

My mother lost her virginity in the Arizona desert. She delighted in telling me this story when I was old enough to hear it. Under a desert moon and with a handsome man — maybe more boy — in his early twenties, and a bottle of wine. A rattlesnake interrupted them.

And even though she was a woman in the desert,

when my mother returned home from thousands of miles away, a long and slow journey by train across our vast country, my mother was still a girl. A teenager.

Her parents didn't meet her at the station. They were off somewhere, church business. There was always church business, my mother told me. And so she, home after months in the desert, had to get herself to her house (was it the same house she'd left? Her parents moved when called, parish to parish). She had to wait alone (her older siblings already grown, married and gone) until her parents returned from their business.

When my mother told me this, I was appalled. Didn't they want to see here? Hadn't they missed her? Weren't they worried?

"It didn't matter," my mother said.

We were driving in Vermont when she told me that story, fifty years after her return from the desert. She was showing me the towns where she'd grown up, the house where she'd lived. Places, until then, I had never been.

She looked out the car's window at the river she told me they used to cross on foot when it froze in the winter, a shortcut to school. She told me how her principal, a family man, would go out first after the freeze, testing the ice. Making sure it was safe for the children.

Among the letters and papers, is an order form to Montgomery Ward, a handwritten shopping list of items to be sent from Chicago, just a few miles from where I sit now as I write this, to Korea. "Auto hat" in navy. Bathing suit. All sorts of stockings in various sizes, materials, and colors. A "low bust" something or other, I can't read the word there, but squeezed on the same line: "figure" and "corset." "Home games," quantity one, price fifty cents.

Tennis slippers and tennis balls. And rubber sheeting for a dollar-twenty-nine. The practicalities of their Korean life. Goods. Garments and games.

An excerpt from a letter my grandfather's aunt sent to Korea: "Tony got killed Wednesday week before last. The little fellow had gone out to the hayfield with your father. He had been working so hard to dig out a groundhog and became so hot and tired that he lay down in the shade of the wagon on which they were loading hay to haul it in. The wagon ran over him and he died next morning. We put him in a nice little box and buried him in the shade of the twin maples north of the garden. And none of us felt ashamed of the tears we shed for poor little faithful Tony. It just seems so lonely. He was after your father all the time like a little boy. I wish we could get a nice fox terrier. It doesn't seem right without a dog."

And at its end: "Please write more often and let us know if something is wrong."

What must it have been like to await word for weeks, sometimes months, from someone on the other side of the world? To read of accomplishments and loss from folded sheets of handwritten notes, struggling to make out the words among the pen marks? And here are my grandfather's letters, typewritten mostly, carbon copies on something like tissue paper, wrinkled and disintegrating at the edges, other words and letters showing through from the flipside, a way to conserve paper, to use everything since they were so far away from everything, shops and supplies and conveniences.

A short note among those from Korea. This one to New York. The National Cloak and Suit Company. A note that must have accompanied a pair of shoes, style number something or other, size something, chosen from a catalogue. "Please send one size larger," my grandfather requests. How many weeks did he have to wait for a new pair of shoes?

My grandfather was an inventor. I remember this from when I was a girl and he and my grandmother lived in Wapakoneta, Ohio (the hometown, by the way, of Neil Armstrong, the first man to walk on the moon, another place I have never been). My grandmother by then was a double amputee, diabetes, I think, and her days were divided between bed and wheelchair. My grandfather rigged up a complicated pulley system to help him get her from one spot to the other. She'd sit high in her bed and hold on to this thing that looked like a trapeze, her upper body still strong. My grandfather would hoist her onto the rig then, and lift her some, and together they would get her into the chair.

There is a photo among these Korean ones of my grandfather's motorcycle with some huge thing in the sidecar. A machine, big as a boy. It's a cook stove, I discover from his letters. Something he's made to carry on his journeys, fueled by wood, a way to have hot meals on the road.

A small thing I remember among my grandfather's inventions: an empty thread spool with a nail hammered in it and bent parallel to the spool's curved surface. He used this as a toothpaste roller, threading the emptying tube between nail and spool, and winding it flat to get every bit of toothpaste out of it.

I know these things he made are available now, versions of them, and conveniently so. Toothpaste rollers, hospital pulley systems, portable cook stoves. Invented by others, not my grandfather, others who profited from their innovation and industry. But I wonder, was anyone more satisfied by a hot meal cooked on his portable stove than my grandfather would have been after hours riding the crooked trails over Korean hills and rivers in the early 1900s? Or more satisfied—no, delighted—than I was as a little girl, as I watched the white worm of Pepsodent issue from its tube while I wound it tighter and tighter around the spool of my grandfather's invention?

In the last year of my mother's life, months before I would go through her things, before I would find these letters and files and photos, we brought hospice into her home. They did what they do to get started, visited and asked questions and made a plan and told us the rules. No medical intervention, they said. Something for the pain, for comfort, but nothing to prolong things. It seemed both reasonable and not: no IV if she got dehydrated? Nothing for her body's deep, unquenchable thirst?

And they asked if she wanted a chaplain to call.

"No," she said emphatically. I was surprised.

We sat in her living room, Mom in her soft, nubbed reclining chair, me on the blue velvet couch, the hospice worker on a wooden dining chair with her back to the view from the balcony, through the tall, tall trees that grew up from the courtyard below. It was July and early in the afternoon, the sun wouldn't set for hours.

When my father died in my fifteenth year, I struggled with heaven, with hell, and I told my mother about the Moonie girl I'd met, I told her about my fears.

"Is that what you really think?" she asked me back then when I said I knew my father was going to hell because he was an atheist, an unrepentant sinner. Hell despite his kindnesses, despite his social conscience. And she said something like, "Oh, darlin'." She looked sad. "I don't think that's what will happen."

She didn't say any more, and I didn't ask; it hurt enough for us to get this far in the conversation, we both cried so easily. But I always thought that she had another idea about heaven, about hell. About God. I always believed that she believed, even though she no longer practiced any religion (an interesting word for this: practice, never a master, forever in training).

So, just a few short months after the hospice social worker had come to survey us, to make a plan, my mother was close to the end. We all knew. She knew. The phone rang.

"Yeth," she said into the receiver. She didn't have her teeth in, they hurt her now, her mouth was raw and dry all the time.

"Yeth," she said again. I heard the creep of annoyance in the edge of the word; a telemarketer, I thought, someone invading our little time left.

"Who told you to call?" she said. And she twisted at the buttons of her robe, an anxious fidget that I've inherited: twisting, tapping, fluttering. "I thaid I don't want to thpeak with you."

Who is it? I mouthed when she looked at me, but she waved away the question.

"How dare you call me when I thaid I don't want to thpeak with you." She pulled the phone away from her ear and looked at the keypad, searching for the disconnect button, pushing a number first, or the pound key; the touchtone sang loudly through the receiver.

"Damnit," she said, and found the right button. "It wath that chaplain," she said. "From the hothpith. I hung up on him." And I could see that she was angry, her fingers tapping and twisting on her lap. With no real handset and phone cradle to slam it into, hanging up on the man brought her little relief.

I go through these boxes of letters and photos over and over again, looking for what I don't yet know, what I might have missed. I am looking for my mother and for her father, my grandfather, for who I am because of them. I am looking for my place here among these letters, the photos, the stories and memories they conjure. I am looking for my father, too—fathers and daughters—I understand now, even though he isn't in these boxes. I don't think of myself as one of those sorts of people who ponders the big questions, but I can't deny that I am looking for the big answers.

My mother believed in sentences. She believed in words, in stories. When she was a little girl, nine years old, she had an assignment to write about her best friend. The family was back in the States by then, but hadn't fully settled, had already moved once or twice. My mother didn't have a best friend. Often the new kid, always a PK (preacher's kid), many years younger than her closest sibling. I imagine she was lonely often, "the other" still. She was a toddler in the Orient, and a girl in a small town in a vast country where people spoke the language she knew, but had memories she didn't. So she read books. Lots of them, and always. A pastime her father and mother encouraged (she told me about how the family read *Les Miserables* by Victor Hugo out loud together in the evenings) and a pastime she loved.

My mother's best-friend essay was about her bookcase. It was made of bamboo and carried across the world on a ship from Korea, placed in her room and filled with books, the first iteration of her serious habit of keeping. The bookcase held what made her happiest, was home to her closest friends. How many times did she tell me this story, the one about her own story, and about a teacher who read it and loved it, who encouraged her to keep writing?

We visited that teacher on our trip to Vermont. The woman must have been in her nineties, but she knew my mother still. She had the dozens of travel books and geography texts that my mother had written and sent her copies of once they were published. They shared memories, these two, mother and teacher, while we sat in what the teacher called the parlor—a slightly formal room with doilies on the arms of chairs and a smell like dust and liniment.

"I still remember your story about your bookcase," my mother's teacher said and my mother nodded and smiled.

Have I said yet that the bookcase, my mother's best friend, is my bookcase now? Have I said yet that it has moved around the Midwest with me, sat in my bedrooms, my living rooms, my kitchens, and now in my bright and airy Chicago sunroom where I sit to write in my journal?

"Over the Backbone of Korea" is the name of an article my grandfather sent to *Motorcycling and Bicycling Magazine.* Among his letters I find one to the editors of the magazine, a thank you for their having published another article he'd sent them and a cover letter to this one, this "Backbone" one that was (used to be) "enclosed herein." And it is here, in this eager and hopeful letter to an editor that I find my place, next to my grandfather. Not my grandfather the missionary, not my grandfather the motorcyclist, not even my grandfather the father. My grandfather the writer. The one who tells stories and writes them down, who holds the stories out to others with slightly shaking hands: read this, will you? Please? And if by some chance you do, and you like it, find it interesting, perhaps you will share it with others.

And here, too, in this place of writers, my grandfather, me, is my mother between us. A travel writer with hundreds of articles and dozens of books to her credit. A woman who was drawn to travel to places she'd never been since she was a baby in Korea, a toddler in Japan, a child in Vermont. And drawn, too, to write it down.

Here we are, my mother, my grandfather, me, going places. Here we are, side by side, climbing the crooked trails.

FINDING MY FATHER AND THE FBI

I am certain I know where to find it; I can see it in my mind. It is in that basket where I keep old magazines, in the sunroom. Or maybe it is in the file box in the back bedroom. Maybe in the drawer near the loveseat or under the side table next to the couch.

There really aren't all that many places to look, and yet...

My father's FBI file came to me by way of my half-brother Wesley, who got it from my other half-brother Paul. I'm trying to think when I received it in the mail. 2008? 2009? Or was it after my (full) brother Roger died? When we, full and half-siblings were reaching out, grabbing what we could of what was left. And I read it, quickly then, because I was just curious, not too much, but enough to see what I might find out about him, my dad, in this way. See, I thought I knew him, knew his story, even this story, the FBI's one about him being a threat to national security. And so I didn't read very closely. And after I'd read it once, I stashed the file away. Somewhere.

Here is what I know for certain, what I have always known: my father had two families. Not at the same time, but overlapping a little. Married once and father of three boys (my half-brothers). Married a second time and father of three more boys (my full brothers) and then me. Seven children altogether; five of us left now. I call all of my brothers just that, brothers, full or half.

My father died when he was fifty-five years old. I was fifteen years old. I am fifty-five as I write this. Four decades.

FBI files are cool. They look like what you might expect them to look like: crummy photocopies with lots of things blacked out and blurry. In my father's case, pages of notes from the forties, the fifties, the sixties. I can't recall if there were any from the seventies, would there have been? By then he was on his second family, his second life, just a middle-aged suburban guy, four kids and a cat and a dog and a mortgage and two cars in the garage and a camper in the driveway. An organic garden in the backyard: cornstalks that grew messily among the neat parcels of lawn adorned with prim little flower beds that made up our neighborhood. I don't think our neighbors liked the garden, or the cornstalks. Or the large and fly-buzzed compost heap in what was once our sandbox, a plaything too childish for any of us when we first moved into the low-slung contemporary house with four bedrooms and a den and two bathrooms and a Florida room and a quarter-acre lot. I was nine then. Roger was eleven. Don and Allen (also full brothers) were teenagers.

What I can remember from the FBI file is that my half-brother Paul had written in its margins here and there, adding commentary. Clarifying what was blacked out, adding what wasn't said. Stuff about his mom (the person, I've come to believe, who first put the FBI on

Dad's tail), my father's first wife, a woman he married when he was too young, too poor, too unsure of himself to know anything different—that's what men did then, married the women they slept with. Stuff about Paul himself, his brothers (my half-brothers). "Finally, I found me!" or something like that scribbled in one place, Paul recognizing himself in the description of one of my dad's sons. And when I read the file, it was Paul's words in the margins that were most interesting to me, even more so than what the FBI had to say. Why is that, I wonder. Perhaps because Paul at least knew the man who was our dad. He knew him in a very different way than I did, there are twenty some years between us. Paul was a man with his own family when our father died. He wasn't just a witness to my dad's life, he was a participant. What he said mattered to me.

If I can find the damn thing, the sheets and sheets of photocopies gathered together and stashed away in my apartment somewhere, it will be Paul's margin notes I will reread first.

What I sort of remember, but maybe don't entirely because some of it had to be before I was born: Paul coming to live with us when he was a young man, his going to college in the city. Paul and Dad being drinking buddies, not just father and son. Paul and Dad, both newspaper guys at one time or another, writers, working together on story ideas. Paul—having moved in his thirties to a tiny town in northern Wisconsin, a rural route for his address—coming back to the suburb where we lived when my father died, and getting lost for hours (was it hours?) just a mile away from our house because everything had changed so much. Getting lost in a familiar place. I know that feeling.

My dad and I were close, as close as a middle-aged father and teenaged daughter could be back in the seventies, an era when fathers worked all the time and wouldn't think of missing a client dinner or late-night meeting to go to a daughter's play or a parent-teacher conference. You know that show *Mad Men*? My dad was that kind of dad. Not the philandering kind (at least not during my lifetime, I don't think) but the hard-working, hard-drinking, suit, tie, Brylcreem kind of dad. A stop-at-the-bar-before-he-came-home-for-dinner, a bourbon-at-lunch kind of dad. Read-the-newspaper-on-the-train-to-work-from-the-suburbs kind of dad; office-in-the-city kind of dad. Smoke-too-much, work-too-much, drink-too-much, weigh-too-much, massive-coronary-in-a-Stop 'n' Shop-on-the-way-home kind of dad.

The FBI file says things about my mother, too, but I don't recall exactly what. Did it name her? Or does it just tell of how my father left his first wife for this other woman, one interested in unions and socialism and Communism like he was. A woman, no doubt, the FBI considered a national threat as well. Certainly a woman who was a threat to my father's first wife, to his first family.

He was a different kind of dad then, no doubt, during his first family years. The FBI file, the one I can't lay my hands on right now, made that clear. He didn't know how to be a family man, I don't think. He had been a farm kid who wanted to be something else, something important. So he was never around when the FBI tried to speak with him, off union building and rabble rousing, his wife and children home alone for days, weeks. My half-brother

Wesley, a poet, writes poems about this dad (his dad, not my dad, at least not the one I knew). The dad who left his family, my half-brothers and their mother, behind when he tried to save the world or something, left them behind when he took up with my mom (who also wanted to save the world). I write stories about him, my dad, essays like this, and fiction. Only the fathers in my fiction aren't exactly like my dad; they are mostly there in the story for a little while, and then they are gone.

Okay, they are exactly my own dad that way. There, then gone.

Where is that file?

What isn't in the file, but what I was told: my mother and father fell in love at first sight. My mother told me this; my father told me this. This is a story I know for sure. He was speaking at an event in a tiny college in Vermont. Someone my mother knew who was involved in labor relations suggested she come to hear this man—my father, but not yet—speak. She walked into the hall where a group was gathered. She had on a beret. It was snowing. She had snow in her hair and on her shoulders and he saw her and he knew. And she knew. That's what they told me. It didn't matter that he was already married, not to them at least. They knew.

This is how things become true: in the file, early on, there is an allegation (presumption?) that my dad absconded with something like 500 bucks from a guy he worked for in Detroit. And for years after, that small detail was brought up again and again in those FBI pages. And with each retelling it became less allegation and more fact until finally, the FBI just started to call it a theft and my father was no longer innocent until proved guilty; he was, according to the file, just plain guilty.

When my poet-brother Wesley was working on his memoir, he came to visit me, to read letters and documents my mother had saved and that were (after her death) passed on to me. We rode in the backseat of a car my husband drove through the country one afternoon; Wesley's wife sat shotgun up front. We were talking about my dad, his dad, our dad, as we had been for days by then. Rather, Wesley was asking me questions — and if the answer I gave didn't exactly match the information he already had, or the way he wanted the history to be, he'd challenge me. And suddenly, unexpectedly, I was crying. The green countryside swept past on either side of the gray strip of highway, and I couldn't stop sobbing. "What do you want me to say?" I remember asking Wesley, struggling to keep my voice steady, my tears from falling. "I'm sorry if it's not what you want to hear. But this is how I remember it." He cried then, too; for me, probably, more than for my dad, our dad, his dad, the one who left him (abandoned him) when he was a child. What were we talking about just then, the moment before I cried? And what did we talk about after? Does what we said matter?

So back to how things become true: the retelling of things, over and over, fact or fiction, makes them more solid, permanent. Am I the only writer who, while making story, stops to wonder: "Did that really happen?" Or "Did I just make that up?" Or "Was that real?" The lines get blurred sometimes, the things we know, the things we create. The things we write down on paper. And maybe that is part of it, too, of what makes things true: words on the page, the act of capturing in ink on paper these myths, stories, allegations. I saw Dorothy Allison read from a novel and talk at the Harold Washington Library once and someone asked her that question readers always have for writers: "Was that story true?"

"Aw, honey. It's all true," she said. "It's fiction, but it's true."

It's true that my dad was followed by the FBI. He was a card-carrying Communist who was a union rabble-rouser in the forties and fifties. To some, that meant he was a national threat: not true, not really. He was a bad father to his first batch of children, and — mostly — a better father to his second; this is true. The file, what I can remember of it since I can't find it, pieced together bits of his life, mostly from years before I was born. Those bits don't add up to the father I knew, the suburban dad with an organic garden who worked a day job in an office wearing a tie and who mowed his lawn while wearing shiny work pants and black socks and dress shoes on weekends. My dad didn't abandon my family or steal 500 bucks from his boss or plan in secret meetings to overthrow the government with his Commie friends. My dad took the train to work. The Skokie Swift. He sometimes left the office early on summer days to go to a Cubs game. He wrote books with titles like *How to Get a Higher Paying Job Now* and *New Careers for Teachers*. He had nothing to hide, nothing the FBI needed to know.

My parents went to the USSR in the sixties on a sponsored trip by a national association of school board members. (My dad helped my mom get elected to our school board; he wrote her campaign flyers.) This trip behind the Iron Curtain stirred up the FBI, according to the file, years after they had finally realized that my dad was just that, a dad. It was sometime before the trip that the FBI finally got him, followed him and stopped him and "invited" him into a car with a couple of agents so they could interrogate him about—what? I can't remember now what they thought he would know. I recall thinking, as I read this section of the file, that it was like the stuff you see on old tapes from the McCarthy era, them—the agents—asking questions about the people he knew, who was a Communist, who was doing what. But this I remember for sure (I think): my father told them he would not say anything. They had no reason to bother him; he didn't have any information. And even if he did, he would not give them anything. Why did they think he would?

The file said he was "uncooperative."

And so they let him go. And later, when he went to Russia on a sponsored trip, the FBI buzzed about it a little in the file; then they let that go, too. School board. Visits to grade schools. That's all. Nothing new here. No big deal. And less than a decade after that, my father died.

What am I really looking for, I wonder. I've gone through the basket of magazines, the drawer next to the loveseat, the piles of things under the end table, the file boxes gathering dust in the back bedroom and I've found nothing. What am I looking for? It's not the file, I think I know now, not really.

It's him. Forty years after the massive heart attack took my father (have I told you his name? Wilbur Frank McNair, Mac to my mom, to his friends, but he went by Bill McKee for work purposes, or so I was told. That drove the FBI a little crazy, two names, three sometimes) and I am as old as he was when he died. And like it is with the file, I am having a harder and harder time remembering exactly where I've left him.

This is what is true, this is what I can find when I look hard enough, what I remember for certain:

My father liked to cook things. Meatloaf with strips of bacon adorning its top. I see my father at the stove stirring a pot of fish stew made from powder, or chili mac made from scratch.

He had a winter coat bought from a resale shop in Ridgeview (he loved resale shops, he loved bargains in general: bikes from police auctions, slightly used things from yard sales, twofers). It was made of bear skin, and he wore it to Chicago Bears games.

My father grew orchids in a greenhouse behind our home in the suburbs. On Saturdays, we would go to Hausermann's Orchids in Villa Park to buy more. It smelled green and like wet earth there. I still love that smell.

Sometimes he came home drunk and grumbling.

My father could hit a softball all the way to the end of our yard while clenching a cigarette tight in his teeth, squinting through the smoke.

He never ran. Or at least, I never saw him run.

My father and mother too often had screaming fights in the middle of the night, moving from their downstairs bedroom to the kitchen, pouring drinks and rattling ice, while we tried to sleep one floor above them. Now and again I would sneak down the backstairs and hide behind a chair in the living room to try to hear what they were saying. The fights were usually about money. Sometimes about other people — men, women.

He was missing teeth (a farm kid's bad dental hygiene in the first quarter of the last century) but he had a great, craggy smile.

He loved me. He called me "Trish the Dish" and sang Jerome Kern's "All The Things You Are" to me, about me.

There's more, I know, about this man, my father, Wilbur Frank McNair. Bill McKee. Mac. Some of it might be in that file, but most of it won't be.

This is not in the file: the night before the day he died, my father was up for hours writing a long letter to my mother about the exciting possibilities of their lives, of our lives. (The letter may or may not be among my mother's things; I haven't found it, either.) When I went to kiss my dad good-bye before I left for school on the morning of the day he died, he snored through the kiss. "He's dead to the world," I said to my mom.

By that evening, he was.

What more can I tell you? What more do you (I) want to know?

He was a Communist; the FBI had that right.

He was a union rabble rouser; true.

He was not a national threat, unless you consider trying to make the world a better place for workers a threat to the nation. I don't.

He grew up on a farm.

He loved to travel. To visit new places. To meet new people.

He did not believe in God.

He was a tenor.

He was a writer.

He was a husband. Twice.

He — Wilbur Frank McNair, Bill McKee, Mac — was my father.

And this I know for certain: I — writer, storyteller, twice-married traveler — I am his daughter.

ACKNOWLEDGEMENTS

Oh, man. None of this happens in isolation. Writing can be a lonely pursuit, but it is the human connections that give us what we need: stories, support, and courage. I owe so much to my Columbia College Chicago colleagues in the fiction writing program (Shawn, Gary, Ann, Andy, Eric, Joe, Sam, Alexis, and Don), my creative writing colleagues, and especially Betty Shiflett, John Schultz, and my dear friend and mentor, Dr. Randall Albers. My family — what is left of us, me, Don, Allen, Wesley, and Paul — I hold close in these pages and in the real world. I have shared many of these stories with my writing gal pals Gail and Jana, and I am grateful for their audience and friendship. I have been lifted up by so many other writers, but perhaps especially Anne-Marie Oomen, Katey Schultz, Megan Stielstra, Christine Maul Rice, John Mauk, and my friends in Her Chapter.

A number of these essays or excerpts from them have been previously published in various forms, and I am grateful to the editors and publishers of the blogs, journals, and magazines *Sport Literate; The Good Men Project; River Teeth; Hypertext; The Story Prize Blog; EnRoute Magazine; Superstition Review Blog SR2; Critical Arts Journal; Word Riot; The Quivering Pen; Chicago Literati; Fourth Genre;* and *Brevity;* the anthologies *Briefly Knocked Unconscious by a Low-Flying Duck; The View from Here; Family Stories from the Attic;* and *We Speak Chicagoese;* and the textbooks *Short Circuit: A Guide to the Art of Short Story*

Writing; Culture: A Reader for Writers; and *The Truth of the Matter: Explorations in Creative Nonfiction.* Thank you Abby Sheaffer, Chelsea Laine Wells, Vanessa Gebbie, Dinty W. Moore, Joe Mackall, and Jotham Burrello. Side Street Press brings this all together for me and for you; thank you so much to Dennis Foley, Bill Donlan and the gang, and to Linda Naslund who wields a blue pencil like no one else can.

Further thanks to the administration of Columbia College Chicago for leave to complete this project; the Illinois Arts Council for a number of IAC Fellowships and Literary Awards in support of this work; to the Glen Arbor Art Association, Interlochen College of Creative Arts, and the very wonderful Ragdale Foundation for residencies that gave me a room of my own in which to write.

And to Philip Hartigan. Yes. Thank you, Philip. Thank you.

To contact Patricia Ann McNair or to obtain information about her upcoming readings and events, please go to:

www.patriciaannmcnair.com

BOOKS BY SIDE STREET PRESS

The Drunkard's Son by Dennis Foley

Echoes from a Lost Mind by Carl Richards

We Speak Chicagoese — stories and poems by Chicago writers, edited by Bill Donlon, et al

And These Are the Good Times by Patricia Ann McNair

forthcoming

Model Child by R.C. Goodwin

SIDE STREET PRESS — massaging brain cells one Chicago book at a time.

Side Street Press is dedicated to publishing thought-provoking works of literary fiction and nonfiction featuring Chicago prominently on the page.

www.sidestreetpressinc.com
info@sidestreetpressinc.com